BACKPACKER

The Magazine Of Wilderness Travel

Desert Sense

BACKPACKER
The Magazine Of Wilderness Travel

Desert Sense

CAMPING, HIKING & BIKING IN HOT, DRY CLIMATES

Bruce Grubbs

THE MOUNTAINEERS BOOKS

THE MOUNTAINEERS BOOKS
is the nonprofit publishing arm of The Mountaineers Club,
an organization founded in 1906 and dedicated to the exploration,
preservation, and enjoyment of outdoor and wilderness areas.

1001 SW Klickitat Way, Suite 201, Seattle, WA 98134

BACKPACKER
The Magazine Of Wilderness Travel

135 N. Sixth St.
Emmaus, PA 18098

First edition, 2004

Published simultaneously in Great Britain by Cordee, 3a DeMontfort Street, Leicester, England, LE1 7HD

Manufactured in the United States of America

Acquiring Editor: Cassandra Conyers
Project Editor: Mary Metz
Copy Editor: Paula Thurman
Cover and Book Design: The Mountaineers Books
Layout Artist: Mayumi Thompson
Cartographer: Ben Pease
All photographs by the author unless otherwise noted.

Cover photograph: *Hiking on the Esplanade, a remote section of the Grand Canyon in the Great Basin Desert*
Frontispiece: *Pine Tree Arch, Arches National Park, Great Basin Desert*

Library of Congress Cataloging-in-Publication Data
Grubbs, Bruce (Bruce O.)
  Desert sense : camping, hiking & biking in hot, dry climates / Bruce Grubbs.— 1st ed.
    p. cm.
  Includes index.
  ISBN 0-89886-973-0
  1. Desert survival—Handbooks, manuals, etc. 2. Hiking—Handbooks, manuals, etc. 3. Camping—Handbooks, manuals, etc. 4. All terrain cycling—Handbooks, manuals, etc. I. Title.
  GV200.5.G76 2004
  613.6'9—dc22
                              2004013666

 Printed on recycled paper

Acknowledgments

I'd like to thank the many friends I've explored the desert with over the years, including Roger Bleier, Dan Bingham, and Doug Elliott—our high school backpacking clique. Thanks to Larry Treiber, Doug Rickard, Art Christiansen, and Jim Haggart for our many enjoyable desert hikes and climbs.

Special thanks to "Doc," who got me and my friends into desert backpacking.

I especially want to thank my editors, Cassandra Conyers, Mary Metz, and Paula Thurman, and all the fine people at The Mountaineers Books who shaped my rough manuscript into a book.

As always, thanks to Duart Martin for supporting my desert trips and encouraging this project every step of the way.

And finally, my parents, who showed me the beauty of the desert.

Contents

Acknowledgments   5
Preface   11
Introduction   13

Chapter 1
North American Deserts   21
SONORAN   25
MOJAVE   30
GREAT BASIN   34
CHIHUAHUAN   39

Chapter 2
Desert Backcountry   43
WILDERNESS AREAS   43
NATIONAL PARKS, MONUMENTS, AND PRESERVES   44
NATIONAL FORESTS   45
NATIONAL WILDLIFE REFUGES   46
STATE PARKS   46
PERMITS AND REGULATIONS   46
MAPS, GUIDEBOOKS, AND FREE ADVICE   47
MAKING YOUR WAY   49

Chapter 3
Water and Climate   55
HOW MUCH DO I NEED?   55
CARRYING WATER IN YOUR VEHICLE   57
CARRYING WATER ON FOOT OR BICYCLE   57
CACHING WATER   59
FINDING WATER   59
FILTERING AND PURIFICATION   61
CLIMATE AND ELEVATION   64
SEASONS   64
WEATHER   66

Chapter 4
Desert Hazards   69
THE PLANTS ARE OUT TO GET YOU   69
ANIMALS THAT SLITHER AND SKULK BY NIGHT   72
OLD MINES   80
FLOODS   81
HEAT HAZARDS   81
HYPOTHERMIA   83
WIND HAZARDS   84

Chapter 5
Navigation   85
MAP READING FOR DESERT DRIVING   85
MAP READING FOR DESERT HIKING   86
COMPASS WORK   88
SATELLITE ASSISTANCE FOR DRIVING   91
USING GPS WHEN HIKING   95
NAVIGATION FOR BIKING   96

Chapter 6
Gear for the Desert   97
THE TEN ESSENTIALS   98
FOOTWEAR   102
CLOTHING   104
PACKS   107
SLEEPING BAGS AND PADS   110
SHELTER   113
COOK GEAR   116
OTHER IMPORTANT ITEMS   118
PHOTOGRAPHIC EQUIPMENT   119
EQUIPMENT CHECKLIST   122

Chapter 7
Driving the Back Roads and Biking the Trails   125
CAN I GET THERE FROM HERE?   125
PREPARATION   126
SAFETY IN NUMBERS   129
HAZARDS OF THE ROAD LESS TRAVELED   129
FAT TIRES IN THE DESERT   131

Chapter 8

Hiking and Camping in the Desert   135

FIT AND READY   135

PLANNING   136

SITUATIONAL AWARENESS   140

TRAVEL TECHNIQUES   141

GOING YOUR OWN WAY (CROSS-COUNTRY)   142

CAMPING   146

Chapter 9

Surviving the Worst   153

LEAVE PLANS WITH A RELIABLE PERSON   154

LOST   154

INJURY   155

STRANDED   155

SIGNALING TECHNIQUES   156

FINDING WATER   157

SHELTER   161

FOOD   161

Resources   163

Recommended Reading   167

Glossary   168

Index   171

Preface

desert is variously defined as a wasteland, a useless region, or a place that gets less than a certain amount of precipitation each year. Depending on the authority, the precipitation limit for a desert may be set at 12 inches, 10 inches, or 5 inches. For our purposes, a better definition is that a desert is a place where the availability of water controls all activity. Certainly, water is the drop of life for the entire planet, but nowhere is this fact more obvious than in the desert. Every plant and animal that successfully lives in the desert must adapt to the scarcity of water. Even modern human settlement is completely dependent on desert water sources. We engineer massive dams, dredge hundreds of miles of canals, and drill wells thousands of feet deep to get water for our civilization, but in the end, we humans are still as dependent on desert water as our animal cousins.

In the desert, the amount of water you can carry or find controls every aspect of trip planning. This includes choosing where and when to go, following the practices of dry camping, watching the desert weather, knowing how much water to carry in your vehicle and how to carry it, as well as developing the skills for finding desert water and making use of it while on foot or bike. On a day hike or bike ride, you can carry all the water you'll need. On extended treks, this is just not possible since water weighs 8.3 pounds per gallon. You must plan wilderness excursions around springs, rock tanks, and other water sources. As you develop the skills to plan trips and find water in the desert backcountry, you'll find that these skills are useful not just in the classic deserts but also in the mountains, forests, and other well-watered regions that beckon to you.

Bruce Grubbs

A Note About Safety

Safety is an important concern in all outdoor activities. No book can alert you to every hazard or anticipate the limitations of every reader. The descriptions of techniques and procedures in this book are intended to provide general information. Nothing substitutes for formal instruction, routine practice, and plenty of experience. When you follow any of the procedures here, you assume responsibility for your own safety. Use this book as a general guide to further information. Under normal conditions, excursions into the backcountry require attention to traffic, road and trail conditions, weather, terrain, the capabilities of your party, and other factors. Keeping informed on current conditions and exercising common sense are the keys to a safe, enjoyable outing.

The Mountaineers Books

Introduction

I have to admit it right up front. I'm a desert rat. I like places that don't have too much water. Excess water creates excessive vegetation and causes all sorts of other problems—like swamps and mosquitoes. Besides, all that lush foliage blocks the view. And now, I have another confession to make.

When my parents and I first moved to Arizona (I didn't have a choice, you see), I hated the desert. I thought it was stark and ugly. And hot. I missed the tumbling creeks, meandering rivers, crystal lakes, dense forests, towering peaks, and blue glaciers I grew up with. Gradually, though, as I got out into the unspoiled Sonoran Desert of central Arizona, first with my rock-hounding parents, and later with a Boy

Storm, Vermilion Cliffs, Great Basin Desert

Mountain lion, Arizona-Sonora Desert Museum

Scout Explorer post, and finally, with a few good friends, I discovered the magic of the desert. The clear air, the hundred-mile views, day after day of perfect weather, the dignity and order of widely spaced plants, the fantastic flower shows that follow wet seasons, the incredible toughness of cactus that can withstand months without rain, and the astounding variety to be found in a single canyon. My early exploring and backpacking trips were all in the desert because I couldn't get to more distant mountain trailheads. When my friends and I finally did manage a trip in the "real backcountry," as we thought of the forested mountains and plateaus, I felt claustrophobic. I missed those sweeping desert vistas and sunsets that lit up the entire sky from west to east. After that, I eagerly embraced the desert, and I've done so for nearly 40 years now. Don't misunderstand; I enjoy the occasional trip to wetter places as a change of scene. Even in alpine mountains, though, I find myself gravitating to the timberline country, far above the cloying forests.

If you've read this far, you must have a streak of desert rat in your blood as well. If so, you've picked up the right book. My purpose is to show you how to safely enjoy the deserts in all their variety and seasons. I'll share my experience and that of others so that you can learn from our mistakes. I'll describe where and why deserts occur on the Earth, the different desert regions of North America, and explain how to find unspoiled places to explore, bike, and hike. One of the prime symptoms of those who've become desert aficionados is, ironically, an obsession with water. That's understandable, because we are creatures made mostly of water, and we need it to sustain life. I'll show you how much water to carry under different conditions, how to find water in the backcountry, and how to carry it in your vehicle and in your pack. There's an old joke that the desert has only two seasons, cold and hot. Others say that the two desert seasons are wet and dry. Both perceptions are true, and understanding desert seasons and climate is the key to enjoying the desert. Many people are nervous about exploring the desert because they think that the land is covered with sharp, spiny plants and crawling with venomous snakes and other nasty creatures. I'm here to tell you that it's all true. The unique plants and creatures are part of the desert's charm, and the hazards are easy to avoid with knowledge and preparation.

The desert is a big place. The four major North American deserts cover a significant portion of the continent, and permanent human settlement tends to cluster in the cities. Desert backcountry is sparsely populated, and exploring the desert requires serious back-road driving. By back roads I mean largely unmaintained roads. It's not uncommon to drive 50 miles of dirt to reach a trailhead or interesting canyon. I'll tell you how to prepare your vehicle for remote desert roads, and how to avoid getting stuck in deep sand or busting a tire. And I'll help you figure out those confusing mazes of unsigned two-track roads that snake every which way and aren't shown on your map.

Native Americans thrived in the desert on foot, without machinery, or even horses, for thousands of years before Europeans arrived with high technology. Foot travel, whether on a day hike or an extended backpack trip, is among the most intimate and rewarding means of exploring the desert. I'll show you how to pick the right high-tech equipment and clothing, but not too much of it, to have the best of both worlds—a primitive desert experience with the comfort and low impact of modern gear. And I'll discuss the techniques that go with the gear, finding your way on trail and cross country, as well as the special methods for traversing the desert's unique terrain. I'll talk about desert camping and how to pick your site to avoid losing your food to hungry camp-robbing rodents. I'll also tell you how to avoid cold nighttime inversions and how to avoid having your camp swept away by a sudden wall of water. And if a disaster does occur, you'll learn how to survive being stuck on a back road, running out of water, getting lost, and experiencing common desert medical problems.

Although this book focuses on techniques for the North American deserts, the things you'll learn are applicable, with modification, for other deserts of the world, and are useful in wetter regions as well. There are plenty of books on general backcountry and wilderness technique—in this book I focus on the difference that the desert makes rather than repeating all the advice already in print. Refer to the Recommended Reading appendix for books that I recommend.

Leave No Trace
Leave No Trace is a set of principles for minimizing our impact on the land. The backpacking boom of the 1970s showed that even hikers and backpackers can severely degrade the backcountry. Leave No Trace is a joint partnership between the National Outdoor Leadership School and the U.S. Forest Service, Bureau of Land Management, National Park Service, and U.S. Fish and Wildlife Service.

Leave No Trace involves seven principles:
1. Plan ahead and prepare.
2. Travel and camp on durable surfaces.
3. Dispose of waste properly.
4. Leave what you find.
5. Minimize campfire impacts.
6. Respect wildlife.
7. Be considerate of other visitors.

How do the Leave No Trace principles apply to desert exploration? First, recognize that the desert is fragile. It may seem like a harsh and barren environment, but all the North American deserts are teeming with life. That life, both plant and animal, depends on scarce resources, especially water. Any disturbance to soil cover or slow-growing plants can take decades to recover. Tracks are still visible from military training maneuvers carried out in the Mojave Desert during World War II.

Advance planning and preparation for your desert trip is important. For ex-

Opposite: Desert pavement, Eagletail Mountains, Sonoran Desert. Desert pavement takes thousands of years to form and is easily destroyed by bicycles and motor vehicles.

ample, having a comfortable sleeping pad means that you can sleep on sand, gravel, and rock, rather than seeking out fragile patches of grass or duff. Having a good tent or other shelter means that you won't feel the need to dig drainage ditches to keep water from getting into leaky seams.

Watch where and how you walk. In the high deserts of the Colorado Plateau, a black crust is often found on the sandy soil. This cryptobiotic crust is actually a microscopic community of plants that act together to protect the underlying soil from erosion. Once disturbed, it can take decades for the crust to reform. Similar soils are found in many desert areas.

Desert pavement is a layer of stones left on the surface by the dissolving and leaching away of the underlying soil, and by the action of wind in removing loose particles. This protective surface is easily destroyed by off-road vehicle tires, which greatly accelerate erosion. It can take hundreds of years to reform. Stay on existing trails and roads when possible. When you have to walk cross country, stay on sand, gravel, bedrock, or animal trails as much as possible. On fragile surfaces, spread out to avoid creating a trail.

Camping causes the most impact on the backcountry. Your impact can be reduced by camping on hard surfaces or, failing that, camping in previously used sites. Sand and gravel are certainly acceptable, but some of the best campsites are to be found on bare rock. The impact is zero and all you need is a good sleeping pad to make a rock campsite as comfortable as one in deep, soft—and fragile—grass. You'll have to be careful of your tent floor, and anchoring your shelter requires different techniques from forest camping, but the rewards can be immense. I'll expand on minimum-impact camping in Chapter 8.

Disposing of waste properly means carrying everything out. All trash and food scraps must be carried out. Animals will always dig up buried food, and human food is never good for them. Even if they do eat your leavings, they'll make a mess doing it. Such practices attract even more scavengers, which then become nuisances or even dangers for the next campers.

Human waste is a serious problem in the desert. Most desert land managers now recommend carrying out all used toilet paper, and some areas require that human waste be packed out. Otherwise, dispose of human waste by selecting a spot at least 200 feet from springs, creeks, lakes, and other open water. Dig a small pit 6 to 8 inches deep, into but not below the organic layers of the soil. Avoid sandy, barren soil whenever possible. Pack out your toilet paper. Carry a set of nesting zippered plastic bags and some baking soda to cut the odor (this also works if you have to carry out your waste as well). Don't burn toilet paper—many desert wildfires have been started this way, including the fire that burned the gorgeous Deer Creek Valley in the Grand Canyon. When finished, replace the soil and the ground cover as much as possible. Don't cover the site with a rock because that inhibits natural decay.

Leaving what you find should be a principle that's easy for a wilderness traveler to apply. After all, presumably you're there to enjoy the desert in a wild, untouched state. Common sense and courtesy mean you would leave everything as you found it for the next visitor to enjoy. It's especially important to leave archaeological ruins and artifacts undisturbed. Moving or removing an artifact destroys its context, which is a major piece of the prehistoric puzzle. Federal and state laws prohibit disturbing archaeological and historical sites, and all natural features are protected in national parks and monuments.

Campfires are prohibited in some desert areas, such as Grand Canyon National Park, because there is little wood to burn and because campfire scars last for hundreds of years. Campfire scars are still visible from the Anasazi people who lived in the Grand Canyon more than a thousand years ago! In general, you should avoid building campfires in the desert. If you have good equipment and clothing, you'll have no trouble staying warm without a campfire. If you must build a campfire, select a site where the ground is free of duff, grass, and all other flammable material. Then dig a pit into mineral soil, using the dirt to form a berm around the fire pit. Keep your fire small—it's easier to cook on a small fire and small fires don't have as much tendency to throw sparks onto your equipment. Before leaving camp, even temporarily, put your fire out by stirring in dirt and mixing until the fire is cool to the touch. That means you should be able to put your hand into the ashes— if you can't, the fire *is not out*. Fires can escape from under a layer of dirt, so never

Campfire built in a sand pit, with dirt clods for a fire ring

Afterwards—the fire is put out, the clods are broken up, and the sand is replaced.

bury a fire before it is out. Before you leave your campsite, use the remaining dirt from the pit to cover the pit and restore the surface to as natural a condition as you can. Never use rocks to construct a fireplace. The fire scars on the rocks last just about forever, and some rocks explode when heated in a campfire.

Respecting wildlife means observing animals from a distance and not feeding them, either accidentally or deliberately. Use binoculars for viewing and a long telephoto lens for photographing wildlife. Desert backcountry and wilderness areas are the last refuge for many animals and plants whose habitat is being steadily destroyed by human development. Treat the desert as you would someone else's home—which is exactly what it is.

Other visitors to the backcountry are there for the same reasons as you—to enjoy a primitive experience away from the pressures of modern life. Avoid overcrowded places and times as much as possible. Camp well out of sight of trails; avoid the use of camp lanterns; and pick muted colors for your tent, pack, and outerwear. Don't make unnecessary noise while hiking or in camp. (Grizzly bear country is an exception, where you want to make noise as you hike to avoid startling a bear, but sadly, grizzlies have long been extinct from the American Southwest.)

Reader Participation

The desert will give you many years of pleasure as you become a seasoned desert explorer. You can give something back. First of all, support the conservation organizations that work to protect America's remaining desert wilderness. And you can become even more active by participating in trail construction and maintenance. Land management agencies, always hard-pressed for money to maintain trails and campgrounds, rely on thousands of hours of volunteer work each year.

We want your feedback on this book's content and presentation so we can improve it for future editions. Send your comments to The Mountaineers Books, 1001 SW Klickitat Way, Suite 201, Seattle, WA 98134, or visit The Mountaineers Books' website at *www.mountaineersbooks.org* or *Backpacker* magazine's website at *www.backpacker.com.*

Chapter 1

North American Deserts

Deserts cover about 14 percent of the world's surface, so they represent a significant portion of the Earth. The major deserts of the world are the Sahara Desert of northern Africa, the Australian Desert, the Arabian Desert, the Turkestan, the North American Desert, the Patagonia Desert of Argentina, the Thar Desert in India, the Kalahari and Namib of southern Africa, the Takla Makan of China, the Iranian Desert, and the Atacama-Peruvian Desert of South America. Of the world's deserts, the Sahara is the largest at 3.5 million square miles; the North American Desert is fifth in size at 500,000 square miles.

The world's major deserts occur approximately along the tropic of Cancer and the tropic of Capricorn, at 23.5 degrees north and south latitude. It's no accident that deserts occur along the lines that divide the mid-latitude temperate zones from the equatorial tropics. Global circulation patterns in the atmosphere produce regions of descending air north and south of the equator. Strong solar heating along the equator causes air to rise, cool, and lose its moisture in the form of rainfall, which produces the tropical rain forests of the world. As the global circulation carries the air away from the equator, it starts to descend, which heats and dries the air, and creates, in a general way, the arid regions of the world.

Although all deserts share one common factor, aridity, they are all different. Variations in geology, geography, and climate cause each desert to have its own

Pronghorn, Great Basin Desert

distinct character. Plants and animals have developed along separate, though sometimes parallel, evolutionary lines in each desert region.

There are four major North American deserts: the Sonoran, the Mojave, the Great Basin, and the Chihuahuan. Although all four deserts are located in western North America, they differ in their plant and animal communities, geology, landforms, and climates. Because of these factors, the four deserts are distinctly different from each other. But the exact boundaries of the deserts are hard to define because they blend into each other and the surrounding nondesert regions. Even the boundary of the North American Desert as a whole is difficult to pin down, except where there is an obvious, sharp change such as an ocean or a mountain range.

The Chihuahuan Desert covers a large portion of northeastern Mexico, a small section of southwestern New Mexico, and a portion of the southeast corner of Arizona. It blends into the Sonoran Desert on its northwest margin. The Sonoran Desert covers most of northwestern Mexico and Baja California, the southwest third of Arizona, and part of the southeastern corner of California. The Sonoran blends into the Mojave Desert along its northwest border. The Mojave covers a large piece of southeastern California, a sliver of northwestern

Opposite: Yucca and granite boulders, Providence Mountains, Mojave Desert National Preserve

Bobcat, Arizona-Sonora Desert Museum

Arizona, and the southern tip of Nevada. Here it blends into the Great Basin Desert, which covers the rest of Nevada, the southeast quarter of Oregon, southern Idaho, the southwest corner of Wyoming, western and southern Utah, and portions of northern Arizona.

These deserts occur primarily because moisture-bearing storms from the Pacific Ocean must cross one or more high mountain ranges before reaching the interior regions. The mountains wring most of the moisture out of the maritime air as it moves generally eastward, creating a rain shadow. As the drier air descends the lee slopes of the mountains, the air heats more rapidly than it would if it was still wet, which raises the average temperature of the continental interior. What little moisture remains tends to fall on the desert mountain ranges, leaving the desert valleys even more parched. Because of the southerly latitude, the lack of cloud cover, and the dry, clear air, sunshine is far more intense in the interior than it is in more temperate climates along the coast and farther north. All these factors combine to create a large arid region centered on the southern portion of the intermountain west. Farther east, moisture is able to make end runs around the mountains, especially from the Gulf of Mexico, and the climate gradually becomes wetter. Other factors in the formation of the North American Desert are sheer distance from maritime moisture and cold ocean currents along the coast.

Sonoran

Covering most of northwestern Mexico and southwestern Arizona, the Sonoran Desert is the hottest and at the same time the lushest of the North American deserts. It ranges in elevation from just below sea level to nearly 4,000 feet, and averages about 2,000 feet. Small parallel mountain ranges separated by broad valleys characterize the Sonoran Desert. The northeastern portion of the Sonoran, in central

Widely misused as the symbol of the North American Desert, the saguaro cactus is actually found only in portions of the Sonoran Desert and not at all in the Chihuahuan, Mojave, or Great Basin Deserts.

Arizona, is the most mountainous. Here the ridges are closer together and reach nearly 8,000 feet along their crests, which create islands of pine and fir forest above the surrounding desert valleys. Large areas of the southern Sonoran desert are volcanic, featuring cinder cones, eroded volcanoes, basalt lava flows, and calderas.

Some sections of the Sonoran get no rain at all for several years in a row, while others get snow every winter. Such a wide variation in climate is caused by the fact that the Sonoran has two moisture sources, which give much of the desert two wet seasons. During the North American Monsoon of late summer, moisture moves northwest from the Gulf of Mexico and triggers afternoon thunderstorms. Because the Sonoran Desert is relatively far from the Gulf of Mexico, the thunderstorm activity is erratic, especially in the Arizona-California section. Thunderstorms will occur regularly for several days, and then the moist air mass will retreat into Mexico, causing a dry period of several days or a week. Even when daily thunderstorms are occurring, the actual area wetted by rain is small. Moist air also reaches the Sonoran Desert in the form of winter storms arriving from the Pacific. The coastal ranges in southern California are lower than their northern counterparts, and more of the maritime moisture survives to reach the desert. Because of the summer and winter wet seasons, there's a lot of variety in the Sonoran plant life.

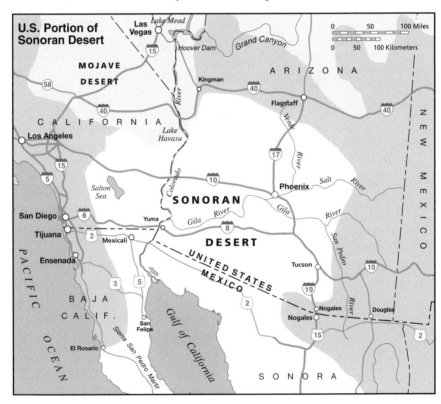

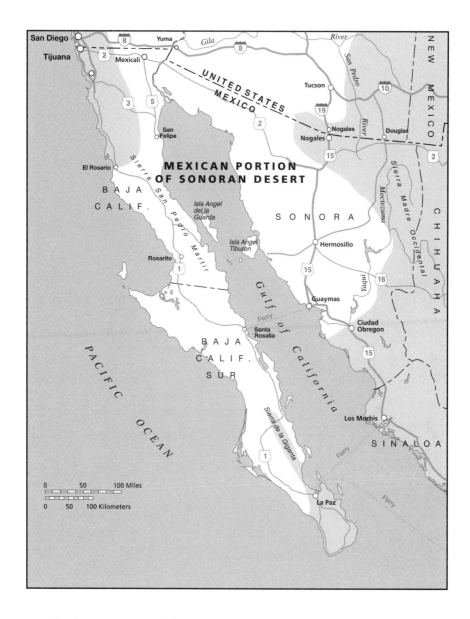

The distinctive plant of the Sonoran Desert is the saguaro cactus, which reaches 30 feet and grows in widely spaced "forests." Although the giant saguaro cactus is the popular symbol of the North American Desert, saguaros actually grow only in favored portions of the Sonoran Desert, and not at all in the other three North American deserts. Saguaros can grow as tall as 30 feet and have a large but shallow root system that efficiently collects moisture after rainfall. The plant survives long dry periods by storing the moisture in its pulpy interior. The tough, pleated skin

Coyote, Arizona-Sonora Desert Museum

expands as the plant takes in water; the waxy skin retards evaporation; and rows of sharp, stiff spines along the ribs discourage most animals from chewing their way into the moist interior. You'll find many other cactuses in the Sonoran, ranging from the lowly pincushions and hedgehogs to the medium-size chollas and barrel cactus and the many-stemmed organ pipe cactus.

Small trees including paloverde, mesquite, ironwood, and smoke trees grow along the dry washes, where groundwater lies close to the surface. Paloverde, which means "green stick" in Spanish, has an interesting adaptation to the harsh climate. Much of the year the little tree has no leaves at all, and survives by photosynthesis in its stems and trunk. When moisture comes, the paloverde quickly produces thousands of tiny leaves. Like several other Sonoran trees, paloverdes send down tap roots as much as 100 feet to reach groundwater.

Creosote bushes grow widely spaced across most of the Sonoran Desert valleys, with several smaller types of bushes growing in between. During the extreme heat—120 degrees F or more—of late spring and early summer, most of the desert ground between these bushes seems to be totally barren. Yet hidden within the soil are the seeds of an incredible flower show. When winter and spring moisture arrives at the right time and in the right amount, these patient

Shin dagger, a low-growing yucca with numerous sharp, stiff leaves, is common in the Chihuahuan Desert but also ranges into the southeast Sonoran Desert.

plants burst out of the desert soil and cover entire valleys and hillsides with yellow, white, orange, blue, purple, and red flowers. Even skeletal trees such as paloverde cover themselves with thousands of tiny flowers. The desert is alive with the heady aroma of millions of flowers and the hum of insects and hummingbirds taking advantage of the sudden bounty.

Another distinctive Sonoran plant, which is also found in the neighboring Chihuahuan Desert, is the ocotillo. This plant has a dozen or so inch-wide stems that grow upward and outward 8 to 12 feet from a common base. Each stem defends itself with sharp spines and is leafless most of the year. If the ocotillo gets enough moisture during the winter, it will grow leaves and then red flowers during the spring. Ocotillos are very sensitive to local variations in moisture on the rocky hillsides they favor; often plants without leaves will be found close to others that are leafed out and in full flower.

Rodents live in burrows among the low bushes and small trees and are preyed on by foxes, coyotes, and snakes. Poisonous snakes range from the red-, black-, and yellow-banded coral snake to the Mojave rattler, which occurs in several color variations that match the tones of the desert or mountains in which it lives, to the unique sidewinder, which moves sideways across the sandy areas and dunes it inhabits. Nonpoisonous snakes such as racers and king snakes are also common.

The night song of the Sonoran Desert is created by coyotes, singly or in packs. They often sound much closer than they are, but coyotes are not dangerous to humans. One night a friend and I were camped in thick brush. The spaces between the bushes were only large enough for one person's groundsheet, so we were about 50 feet apart. Around midnight I was abruptly awakened by a single coyote singing very close by. When the coyote stopped singing I drifted off to sleep, but soon he woke me up with another burst of caroling. After a few rounds I started to get a bit irritated. I'm sure he or she had no idea we were there, because suddenly my friend bellowed "SHUT UP!" and the coyote stopped in mid-yip. He probably didn't stop running until morning.

Mountain lions range the more rugged mountains of the Sonoran Desert, preying on mule and white-tailed deer. They are solitary and rare, and you'll be very lucky to see one. Bobcats are more common, and sometimes leap onto a road and run in front of a vehicle for a hundred yards before disappearing. Bighorn sheep favor the remotest of the Sonoran ranges and can't handle human competition.

Mojave

The smallest of the North American deserts, the Mojave is also probably the harshest. Most of the Mojave Desert is in southeastern California; it also includes the southern tip of Nevada and a small portion of northwestern Arizona. The Mojave blends into the Sonoran Desert on the south and east and into the

Great Basin Desert along its northern margin. Basin and range topography defines the character of the Mojave. Parallel, north-south trending mountain ranges are separated by wide valleys and basins, as in the Great Basin Desert, but the Mojave is more mountainous. Most of the basins are undrained and runoff ends up in salt flats, typified by the floor of Death Valley. Some drainage does reach the Colorado River, which forms part of the eastern boundary of the Mojave. The parallel mountains and valleys of the Mojave, Great Basin, and portions of the Sonoran Deserts are the result of the stretching of the Earth's crust from east

Joshua tree, Mojave Desert

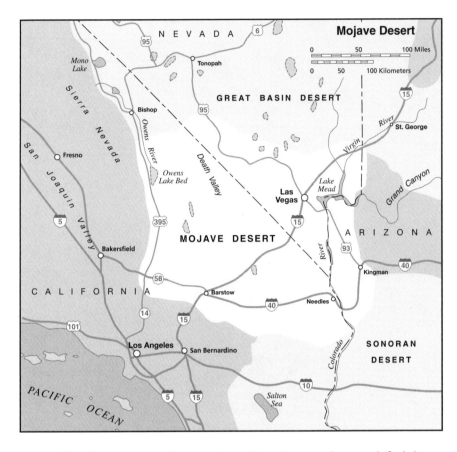

to west. To relieve the stress, the crust is cracking along north to south fault lines. Some of the resulting blocks rise, others sink, and some tilt. Death Valley lies below sea level because the floor of the valley is dropping faster than erosional debris can fill it.

Along some of the fault lines at the base of the mountains, the transition from level desert floor to steep mountain slope is abrupt, like the eastern edge of Death Valley where the Funeral Mountains rise suddenly from the salt flats with no foothills at all. Most ranges have a gentler transition from their surrounding valleys. As the ranges erode, alluvial debris is carried away from the mountains by occasional floods in otherwise dry washes and is then deposited in great fans at the base of the mountains. These debris fans tend to overlap and form broad slopes that run from the steep mountain slopes to the flat valley floor. Called bahadas, these outwash plains appear smooth from a distance but are usually cut by deep ravines and washes. Traveling up or down a bahada is usually easy, but moving parallel to the adjacent mountain range can be tedious as you are constantly dropping into deep washes and climbing up the other side.

Like the Great Basin Desert, the Mojave was much wetter during the last ice age. Large lakes filled many of the now-dry desert basins. Even the floor of Death Valley, now the lowest point in the Western Hemisphere, was a lake. Now, the only lakes you'll encounter are man-made reservoirs or mirages, which are caused by planes of superheated air that reflect the sky like mirrors.

The climate of the Mojave ranges from dry in the western portion to very dry in the eastern. In fact, some locations in the Mojave Desert go years between rains. The little rain that does fall—about 5 inches on the western side and 2 inches or less on the eastern—comes mainly in the winter. Summer thunderstorms do occur, but they are sporadic and mostly along the eastern margin of the desert. Snow falls on the higher Mojave ranges but doesn't last.

Low brush dominates the Mojave Desert, but vegetation is sparser than in the wetter Great Basin Desert to the north. Sagebrush, which covers the Great Basin Desert, makes it down into the northern Mojave, but the most common brush is creosote. Along the salt flats, alkali-tolerant plants such as shadscale take over from the creosote. Contrary to popular impressions, few members of the cactus family survive in the Mojave Desert. The most common are prickly pear and cholla. The signature plant of the Mojave is the Joshua tree, a yucca that grows 10 to 12 feet tall. John C. Fremont, head of the first government survey of the Mojave Desert, called them "the most repulsive tree in the vegetable kingdom." These weird-looking plants are members of the lily family, and the classic stands are in Joshua Tree National Park and Mojave National Preserve.

You may not see much animal life in the Mojave, so it would be easy to conclude that the place is barren. On the contrary, there are desert bighorn sheep, mountain lions, coyotes, deer, many species of smaller mammals such as rodents, plus reptiles such as rattlesnakes and lizards, and many species of birds. Most animals are active only at night, except in the coolest months of the year. During the heat of day, they doze in comfortable burrows and nests, and then come out at dusk to forage and hunt. One animal you are likely to meet in the middle of the night, especially if you camp in popular spots around rocks, is the ringtail cat. This intelligent animal, which resembles a small raccoon, loves to raid your camp and make off with your food and anything else that isn't nailed down.

Several types of woodpeckers and flickers make their homes by pecking out cavities in the Joshua trees. Abandoned nests are then used by many other birds. Above, in the stark blue sky, vultures soar patiently, waiting for some animal to lose the struggle for life and become desert carrion. When these birds spot food, they circle the impending feast, attracting other vultures from miles away. Another carrion eater, the raven, probably regards humans and our highways as the great advance in raven civilization. You'll see ravens pecking away at road kill, but never see a flattened raven. They understand cars and hop or fly out of the way at the last possible second, then immediately return to their meal.

Great Basin

A cold desert, the Great Basin Desert lies at elevations of 4,000 feet or more. It's the largest and northernmost of the North American deserts. It includes all of Nevada except the southern tip, the southeast quarter of Oregon, the southern third of Idaho, a piece of southwest Wyoming, the western and southeastern portions of Utah, and a bit of northern Arizona. The Great Basin grades into the Mojave Desert on its southwest side. On the west, the moist Cascade and Sierra Nevada ranges create an abrupt border. On the north and northeast, the Rocky Mountain ranges in Idaho and Wyoming mark the edge. On the east, the Great Basin Desert comes to an end along the intermountain ranges of central Utah, and on the southeast the desert fades out in the forested central Arizona highlands. This huge area is dominated by two features: sagebrush, which grows in vast stands in the valleys and far up the mountainsides, and basin and range topography. Sweeping

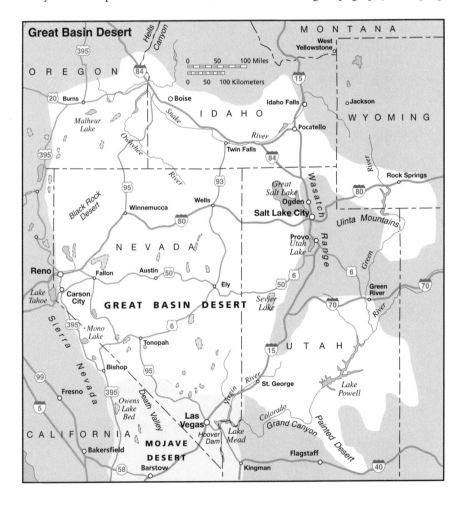

Alpine tundra in the Snake Range, Great Basin Desert. Water can be as scarce here as it is in the warmer desert 6,000 feet lower.

valleys and basins are bordered by dozens of small north-south mountain ranges, which have elevations from 5,000 to 13,000 feet. In the western Utah and Nevada sections of the Great Basin Desert, all drainage flows into interior basins and evaporates. Only in the portions of the desert in Idaho, Wyoming, southeast Utah, and Arizona does runoff make it into a river that eventually reaches the sea.

Great Basin National Park in east central Nevada is a fine example of Great

Basin desert. Here Wheeler Peak rises 7,000 feet above the neighboring 6,000-foot valleys. Even though the Snake Range, containing Wheeler Peak and other peaks above 12,000 feet, was once carved by glaciers, it is now an arid range where bristlecone pines cling to the rocky slopes at timberline. This incredibly hardy tree lives more than 4,000 years in the harshest locations imaginable on Great Basin mountain ranges.

Many other Great Basin mountain ranges rise above 10,000 feet, yet they are all desert ranges. Nearly all the rain and snow in the Great Basin falls in the winter and early spring, and the yearly precipitation ranges from 4 to 13 inches. The mountains attract most of the moisture, and a few live streams run out into the desert basins and evaporate into alkali flats. The mountains and the valleys both receive snow in the winter, and snow usually persists on the higher ranges.

Like the Mojave Desert to the south, the Great Basin was much wetter during the last glaciation. Runoff that now disappears into salt flats or marshes once formed vast lakes that flooded the valleys between the mountains. Ancient Lake Lahontan covered the basins of much of northwestern Nevada, and Lake Bonneville covered much of northwestern Utah. Today, the desert trekker can see clear evidence of these Ice Age lakes in the form of wave terraces carved into the foot of the mountains. It is truly strange to stand on one of these sloping terraces of sand and gravel and imagine the entire valley before you flooded hundreds of feet deep with waves lapping at the shore. Most of the water is gone, but small lakes survive in Nevada, and Utah's Great Salt Lake still covers 1,500 square miles. Since all the water flowing into these lakes evaporates, the lakebeds trap all the dissolved salts and minerals that flow into them. Great Salt Lake is now ten times saltier than the ocean. In the valleys where the glacial lakes completely disappeared, the soil is so salty that only the hardiest of plants, such as saltbrush and shadscale, survive.

Cactus is limited to low-growing prickly pear and hedgehog, because most cactus can't withstand the freezing temperatures of the Great Basin winter. As you climb the mountains, there's often enough moisture to support a pygmy forest of pinyon pines and juniper trees. These trees grow from 10 to 30 feet high and form an open, arid woodland with patches of grass and sagebrush in between. Higher still, hardy trees like mountain mahogany and bristlecone pine cling to the rocky slopes. The wetter ranges have stands of Rocky Mountain or Sierra Nevada trees, such as whitebark and limber pines, Douglas fir, and ponderosa pine.

The vast sage stands make ideal homes for large numbers of rodents. One of these, the kangaroo rat, has made a remarkable adaptation to the desert. It gets all its water by metabolizing its food, and never needs to drink liquid water. I'd like to learn how to do that! Mice and rats are usually plant eaters, but many Great Basin rodents are carnivorous and eat insects rather than plants. There are several species of toads, including the spadefoot toad. In the slickrock canyon country of southeastern Utah,

Opposite: Badlands topography, Great Basin Desert

the spadefoot toad depends on rain pockets in the sandstone for survival. These pockets in the bare sandstone are dry for years and only fill up after a heavy rain. The toads survive for years buried in the silt at the bottom of the dried-out water pockets, until the rains come. Then the spadefoots emerge to mate and reproduce—quickly—before the pocket dries out again. The new generation of toads burrows into the silt to wait for the next rain. If it comes in time, the cycle continues. Otherwise, the colony of spadefoots is wiped out.

Coyotes are found in the Great Basin Desert as they are in the other North American deserts. Coyotes usually prey on mice and other small rodents. Several species of hawk, including the common red-tailed hawk, soar on updrafts and keep a sharp eye out for unwary rodents and pygmy rabbits. Jackrabbits are very common,

Sharp spines and seasonal leaves on ocotillo

and they like to cross dirt roads just as a car comes along. I've been kept alert on many long night drives across the Great Basin by the jackrabbits that suddenly jump out in front of my headlights, run madly back and forth across the road as if trying to commit suicide, and finally dash off into the sage.

Pronghorns love the wide open spaces of the Great Basin, and in fact their survival depends on it. Sharp-eyed and fast runners, these deer-sized animals spot potential predators at distances of a mile or more and move away.

Wild horses once ranged freely across much of the American West. Descendants of domestic horses introduced by Spanish explorers in the sixteenth century, they are now limited to specific ranges in the Great Basin Desert because of their competition with domestic cattle and wildlife.

Chihuahuan

The Chihuahuan Desert lies mostly on a high plateau between two major mountain ranges, the Sierra Madre Occidental on the west and the Sierra Madre Oriental on the east. These mountains remove most of the moisture from air moving from both the Pacific and Atlantic Oceans before it reaches the interior desert. Most of the moisture that does reach the Chihuahuan Desert comes from the Gulf of Mexico, in the form of a seasonal air mass movement called the North American Monsoon. Starting about midsummer, moist air moves northwest over northern Mexico and the southwest United States, triggering afternoon thunderstorms on an almost daily basis. Winters are cold because of the high elevation, from 3,000 to 6,000 feet. Summer rain and cold winters combine to create a single growing and blooming season in late summer.

One of the distinctive plants of the Chihuahuan Desert is candelilla, also known as waxplant because wax is often produced from it. The plant consists of large numbers of thin, waxy, pale green stems. Closely spaced, the stems are leafless and about 2 feet high. Another typical plant is the grayule, which favors the limestone areas of the desert. This low-branching plant's narrow, silvery leaves can be used to make rubber.

Hardy creosote bushes are a dominant plant in much of the Chihuahuan Desert, as well as in the Sonoran and Mojave Deserts. The bush is about 3 to 5 feet tall and grows widely spaced, to make use of what little moisture there is. Creosote bushes excrete an inhibiting chemical from their roots, which prevents creosote seedlings from growing too close to the mature plant. The leaves are small and waxy, a common desert adaptation to conserve moisture. During extended dry periods, most of the leaves drop off, and the plant has an amazing ability to simply endure long periods of heat and dryness. When rain does come, creosote grows leaves again and produces numerous small yellow flowers.

Another common plant, probably too common, is the lechuguilla. An agave, the lechuguilla often covers large areas of the mesas and hills. The narrow, thick, tough leaves grow outward from a common base, and each is tipped with a stiff, sharp spine. Walk through a patch of lechuguilla, and you'll come to appreciate another of its

common names, "shin dagger." The sharp spines often cause painful puncture wounds. Agaves are often thought of as cactus, but they're actually members of the amaryllis family. Agaves save up their energy for years before conditions become favorable for the plant to produce a single, central stalk. This stalk grows rapidly during the summer and produces a showy mass of flowers. After this final effort, the plant dies.

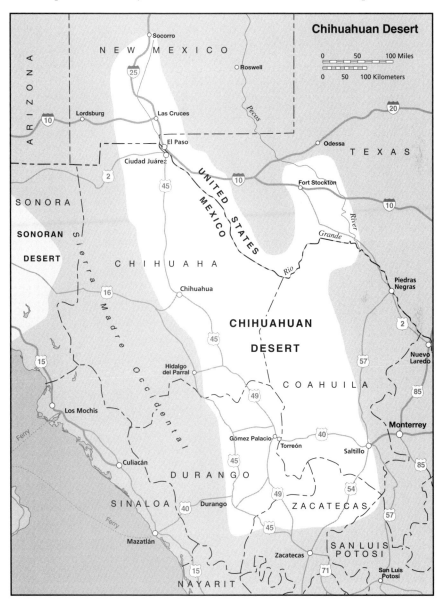

Opposite: Big Hatchet Mountains, Chihuahuan Desert

Yuccas are also common in the Chihuahuan Desert. Sometimes confused with agaves, yuccas tend to have short trunks rather than growing from ground level like the agaves. The leaves of yuccas, while resembling agave leaves, are more numerous and not as tough. Yuccas also have showy flowers and are members of the lily family.

True cactus is more common in the Chihuahuan than in the Great Basin and Mojave Deserts, but it doesn't have the variety and abundance of the Sonoran Desert. You'll find mostly low-growing cactus such as barrel and hedgehog.

Rattlesnakes, lizards, and other reptiles are common in the Chihuahuan Desert. Copperhead snakes are also found here. Rodents, the normal prey of rattlesnakes, are common. Larger animals include coyote, javelina, mule deer, several species of rabbits, kit and grey foxes, badgers, ringtail cats, bobcats, bats, and mountain lions. Bighorn sheep and pronghorn are still found, although in reduced numbers.

Chapter 2

Desert Backcountry

ndeveloped desert lands that are open to the public are generally managed by federal agencies, or in a few cases, by state and local governments. The specific government agency and its management philosophy, as well as public land law, have a definite impact on where you can go and what you can do in the backcountry.

Wilderness Areas

Wilderness areas are part of the National Wilderness Preservation System established by Congress in 1964. These areas have the strongest level of conservation protection and offer the wildest backcountry experience. Wilderness areas have been established on lands managed by all of the federal land management agencies, and the Wilderness Act requires the same protection in each case. The purpose of wilderness areas is to provide a primitive backcountry experience where the impact of humans is essentially unnoticeable, and to preserve plant and animal habitat. Motorized and mechanized transport and equipment, including bicycles, is prohibited. Permanent man-made structures are not allowed, with the exception of administrative structures such as fire lookouts. Roads are not allowed, and trails form the primary transportation network. Some desert wildernesses are very difficult to access because of their size and lack of water sources. An example is the 800,000-acre Cabeza Prieta Wilderness in southern Arizona, which is traversed by only two roads that follow narrow nonwilderness corridors. There are no trails at all and very few roads that even approach the borders. Backpacking across this terrain requires tested navigation skills and certain knowledge of the few water sources. Other desert wildernesses aren't so extreme. The Superstition Wilderness near Phoenix has an extensive, well-used trail network and a relatively large number of springs. In the winter and spring many of the creeks have flowing water, so the Superstitions are a pretty friendly desert wilderness—except during summer.

Large tracts of desert still remain roadless though not (yet) protected under the Wilderness Act. Some of these de facto wilderness areas are designated as Wilderness Study Areas because their wilderness qualities have been recognized by the land agencies. These areas are managed as wilderness while their ultimate fate is debated. Other roadless areas are recognized by citizen groups but not the managing agency. These unofficial wildernesses can be especially rewarding to explore because they don't attract the crowds that the better known areas receive. Utah, for example, has relatively few acres protected as wilderness but more than 9 million roadless acres recognized by federal agencies and conservation groups. Nevada also has vast roadless federal tracts not yet protected by wilderness designation. These are rewarding areas for exploration and present great opportunities for wild-land preservation.

National Parks, Monuments, and Preserves

National parks are the most famous of America's protected lands and are managed by the National Park Service. Americans are proud of their national parks, regarding them as the nation's crown jewels, and are fiercely protective of them. Rightly so, because America invented national parks, an idea that has since spread around the world. Americans also visit their national parks in huge numbers. With some exceptions, you won't find as much solitude in the national park backcountry as you will in a wilderness area. (Many national parks have large areas protected as wilderness as well.) Still, the national parks contain prime desert country that you don't want to miss, such as the desert-to-mountain extremes in Arizona's Saguaro and Grand Canyon National Parks and Nevada's Great Basin National Park, and the slickrock canyon country in Utah's Zion, Canyonlands, Arches, and Capitol Reef National Parks, as well as the classic Mojave Desert in California's Joshua Tree National Park and the Chihuahuan Desert in Big Bend National Park in Texas.

National monuments have been designated for various purposes, including the protection of historical and cultural resources as well as the land itself. The National Park Service, the Bureau of Land Management, and the U.S. Forest Service all have national monuments under their management. Some monuments are highly developed, but most desert national monuments have extensive backcountry. This is especially true of some of the recently designated monuments, such as Escalante-Grand Staircase in Utah and Grand Canyon-Parashant National Monument in Arizona.

Cliff dwelling, Grand Gulch, Great Basin Desert. Prehistoric ruins such as these are fragile and are protected by federal and state laws.

National preserves are managed by one or more of the federal agencies and have been established with a mix of protection levels. A prime example is California's Mojave National Preserve, which was established to protect not only a large portion of the Mojave Desert but also the prehistoric and historic cultural resources within its 1.6 million acres. That's a lot of backcountry to explore, but large portions can be reached by four-wheel drive vehicles and some even on paved roads.

National Forests

Wait. How come I'm talking about national forests in a book about deserts? Well, it's true that most national forests were established to protect tall trees, but not all. Especially in the arid Southwest, national forest boundaries were chosen to protect the vital watersheds that supply water to the cities. The Tonto National Forest, one of the largest in the country, contains large amounts of pinyon-juniper woodland as well as Sonoran desert. The Tonto National Forest was created primarily to protect the watershed for the thirsty and rapidly growing Phoenix area. The popular

Superstition Wilderness as well as other wildernesses, such as the Sierra Ancha and Hells Gate, are in the Tonto National Forest. In general, national forests are managed for multiple uses, and the rangers have the thankless job of balancing land preservation with cattle grazing, timber logging, mining, and recreation. In any case, national forests in the desert regions contain large amounts of prime backcountry that is open for exploration by vehicle, foot, mountain bike, and even by river raft and kayak.

National Wildlife Refuges

National wildlife refuges are managed by the U.S. Fish and Wildlife Service, primarily for the benefit of birds, bighorn sheep, and other wildlife, rather than recreation. Although many refuges are small, some do have extensive areas of desert backcountry and wilderness. An example is the Kofa Refuge and Wilderness in Arizona. Since management is primarily for wildlife, portions of national wildlife refuges may be closed during certain seasons of the year to protect nesting grounds and other sensitive areas.

State Parks

Although most state parks are small, many contain extensive trail systems. These parks are a good way to get started exploring the desert. Most have well-equipped campgrounds and some have other amenities, such as visitor centers and interpretive programs.

Permits and Regulations

As the desert recreation areas become more popular, land managers have to impose more regulations to minimize damage to the resource and impacts on wildlife and vegetation. Less popular areas may have minimal regulations and no permit system, while more popular areas have extensive rules and a strict permit system requiring payment of a fee. When planning a trip, always check the current regulations with the agency unit that manages the area you're going to visit. Often you can do this on the agency's website, but for the most up-to-date information, give them a call. Agency contact information is in the Resources appendix.

Some desert destinations are so heavily used that you must get a reservation in advance, such as Coyote Buttes on the Arizona-Utah border. Another example is the Cabeza Prieta Wilderness, which lies partly within the Goldwater Air Force Gunnery Range, where all visitors must get a permit prior to entry. Overnight backcountry visits in Grand Canyon National Park require a permit and payment of a fee, and some areas in the park require reservations. Other desert regions, especially those managed by the Bureau of Land Management and the U.S. Forest Service, can be visited freely at any time, except during emergencies, such as fire closures.

Maps, Guidebooks, and Free Advice

Maps at various scales and levels of detail are available for the desert areas of the United States. Highway maps are useful for approaching the general area, while more detailed maps are good for navigating back roads for exploration, or to reach a trailhead or area for investigation on foot or mountain bike. The most detailed maps cover a small area and are best used for planning a hiking trip into a specific area.

Most of the land management agencies publish maps of their areas. These vary from general road maps to detailed maps of the backcountry. In all cases, they show ranger stations and facilities, so you'll want to have one for advance planning. See Resources appendix for contact information.

In some cases, individual counties publish detailed road maps showing all the maintained and nonmaintained roads in the county. These vary in accuracy but can be useful for back-road navigation. Contact the local county planning office, which is listed in the government section of phone books, to see what maps are available.

The U.S. Geological Survey (USGS) publishes several series of topographic maps, which show not only man-made features, such as roads, trails, and buildings, but also natural features, such as permanent and seasonal streams and springs. In addition, topographic maps show elevations and the three-dimensional shape of the landscape by means of contour lines. Small-scale maps such as the 1:250000 series (0.25 inch to the mile) and the 1:100000 series (1 centimeter to 1 kilometer) are good for learning the layout of a region and navigating back roads. For cross-country hiking, and even most trail hiking in the desert, you'll need the most detailed and accurate maps published—the 7.5-minute series. At a scale of 1:24000, or 2,000 feet to the inch, these maps are printed in quadrangles that cover 7.5 minutes of latitude by 7.5 minutes of longitude; each sheet represents 54 square miles. The only catch is that the USGS doesn't have a large enough budget to keep

Favorite Desert Hikes
Joint Trail, Canyonlands National Park
Lower La Barge Box, Superstition Mountains
Tanner Trail, Grand Canyon
Paria Canyon, Paria-Vermilion Cliffs Wilderness
Telescope Peak, Death Valley
Mazatzal Divide Trail, Mazatzal Mountains
Nankoweap Trail, Grand Canyon
Bull Pasture, Organ Pipe Cactus National Monument
Heart of Rocks, Chriricahua National Monument
Bisti Badlands, Bisti Wilderness
Ruby Crest Trail, Ruby Mountains

all these maps up to date. Luckily the terrain and vegetation don't change much, so the 7.5-minute maps are still excellent for detailed exploration. Man-made features, such as roads and trails, are often out of date, which has opened up a market for privately published maps.

Based on the government's topographic work, privately published maps are printed in various scales. They vary in accuracy and detail, but are usually revised more often than U.S. government maps. Private maps are generally good enough for road navigation and trail hiking, but you may need the 7.5-minute USGS maps as well.

Topographic maps are also available in digital format for computers, both over the Web and on CD-ROM and DVD discs. Large areas of coverage are available from the USGS and private companies for a fraction of the price of printed maps. Although you can view only a portion of a 7.5-minute map on the computer screen at once, there are several advantages to this high-tech alternative. Most digital maps come with software that lets you measure distances and elevations, plot routes and elevation profiles, and print maps for use in the field.

Superstition Mountains, Sonoran Desert

If you use the Global Positioning System (GPS), you can upload and download GPS positions and routes to your receiver, saving you from tedious manual entry of coordinates.

Trail and back-road guidebooks are available for some desert areas. Such books can simplify your trip planning, but remember that the ultimate responsibility for your safety is yours. Temper the books' advice with knowledge of your own experience and limitations, and that of your group.

There are also general field guides to desert plants, animals, and geology. A little reading through such natural history guides before your trip can greatly increase your appreciation of the desert world. When I'm exploring by vehicle, I always take along the appropriate field guides from my collection. When backpacking, I limit myself to only one book, and then only under special circumstances, such as an unusually good spring flower show or a hike into a wildlife or birding area.

Making Your Way

There are several ways of exploring the desert, mainly by vehicle, by mountain bike, and by foot. Other modes, such as river running and lake paddling, are possible where major rivers and seasonal streams traverse the desert, or where dams form reservoirs. My purpose here is to discuss the advantages and disadvantages of different modes of transportation, saving travel techniques for later chapters.

Driving

You can use public transport, such as airlines, trains, and buses, to reach major desert cities, and you can get to desert parks and preserves in and around these cities by bus or taxi. A few popular desert trailheads are served by shuttle services, but you'll need to drive your own vehicle to explore most desert backcountry and to reach starting points for desert bike rides and hikes.

Conventional wisdom dictates that you must have a high-clearance, four-wheel drive (4WD) truck or sport utility vehicle (SUV) to travel desert roads. There's no doubt that many roads are unmaintained, sandy, and rocky, and a good 4WD truck operated by a driver who knows the limits of the machine can get you safely over remarkably tough terrain. On the flip side, such vehicles are expensive to buy and operate, and many if not most SUVs and light 4WD trucks are marketed to urban dwellers who never venture off pavement. Because a 4WD vehicle designed for hauling heavy loads over rough roads necessarily has a stiff suspension, which gives a harsh ride on pavement, most SUVs have suspensions that are too soft for travel on rough roads. Soft suspensions greatly increase the likelihood of bottoming out on rocks and uneven road surfaces. The tall stance and high center of gravity that is part of the mass-marketing appeal of most

SUVs, along with the soft suspension, create vehicles especially prone to rollover. Another factor to consider is that nearly all SUVs are classified as light trucks and are not as safe as cars, which have more stringent federal safety standards. And finally, many of the SUVs on the market have little more ground clearance than a sedan.

That said, for extended exploration of the desert by road, nothing equals a 4WD vehicle that has been specifically designed and equipped for rough roads. Any 4WD vehicle used for such exploration should have a two-speed transfer case and limited slip differentials. The two-speed transfer case gives you an entire set of lower gears that let you move slowly and even creep over obstacles in the road. Limited slip differentials mean that the opposite wheel on an axle continues to provide traction when one wheel slips. Together, these features mean that you can move slowly without spinning your wheels, avoiding damage to your vehicle and the road surface. Other features such as a vehicle-powered winch can be useful, especially when traveling with two or more vehicles in convoy. Large carrying capacity means you can carry plenty of water, camping gear, and other supplies to make an extended stay in the desert more comfortable.

Notice I haven't said anything about off-road driving. That's because many desert areas are closed to off-road driving, and most of those that aren't should be. Desert soil and plants are extremely fragile. Protective crusts take decades or centuries to form, but once destroyed by a passing vehicle, they leave the desert soil open to rapid erosion. Likewise, most desert plants grow slowly but are easily crushed by vehicle tires. Scars last for decades. Responsible drivers stick to roads.

If your primary desert interest lies in the direction of mountain biking or hiking, then you may not need a 4WD truck. Some desert trailheads can be reached on paved roads, and many more on maintained dirt roads. An ordinary car can reach these trailheads. Many unmaintained roads can be traveled safely by car, if the driver knows how to handle soft surfaces and obstacles. Still, it's much easier to get stuck in soft sand, or damage the vehicle or road, in a high-geared, low-clearance car. A newer class of vehicles, the car-based SUV, offers a compromise between a 4WD truck and a typical car. These vehicles have higher ground clearance than a car, while still maintaining a lower center of gravity than a truck-based SUV. They also get much better gas mileage than large SUVs and trucks. Four-wheel or all-wheel drive (AWD) is common on car-based SUVs, and sometimes you can find features such as limited-slip differentials. Sadly, because marketing is targeting these vehicles at the urban-only market, features like two-speed transfer cases that greatly improve their utility for back-road travel are disappearing from car-based SUVs. But if you mainly need to reach jumping-off points for bicycling or hiking and don't need to haul heavy car-camping loads, a car-based SUV may be a good solution.

Mountain Biking

Mountain bikes with low gearing, high-traction tires and sophisticated suspensions have opened up a whole new world of self-powered desert travel. Although bicycles are banned from trails in designated wilderness areas and national parks, there is much desert backcountry traversed by unmaintained, double-track roads that are ideal for mountain bikes. In certain areas, mostly around desert cities, mountain biking organizations and land management agencies have developed some fine single-track riding. In the backcountry, many desert roads that would be uninteresting or too long to hike are ideal for mountain bike exploration. You can use your truck or car until the road becomes too rough, and then continue on your bike. You can even use the bike as a sort of second-stage vehicle to reach a trail or area that you want to hike. A mountain bike is also valuable as a spare vehicle in the event your motorized vehicle breaks down deep in the desert. Unless the riding surface is too soft, a cyclist can cover several times more distance than a hiker in the same time.

Trail Hiking

You'll find a surprising number of trails in the desert backcountry. Many of the trails were originally built for mining or ranching, and an increasing number are being built expressly for recreation. National parks and designated wilderness areas have the most trails, but you'll also find trails in state parks and national forests. There's a lot of variation in the difficulty of desert trails. Many are well-built, maintained, and signed and are easy to follow, even for a novice. Other trails receive little use or maintenance and can be challenging to follow, even for an expert. USGS topographic maps show trail information in detail, but USGS topo maps aren't updated that often and trails are rerouted or become overgrown with brush. In theory, the "system trails" shown on national park and national forest maps are part of the park or forest's transportation system. Such main trails are used for management purposes, such as field research and fire fighting, and are supposed to be maintained and signed. In reality, trail maintenance budgets fluctuate wildly and a given trail may not have had maintenance for many years. The bottom line is: Don't expect that a trail shown on a map will be in good shape—or even exist. When in doubt, check a guidebook and contact the agency that manages the trail you'd like to use.

Trail hiking is the best way to get your feet wet—or rather, dusty—in the desert. You can get familiar with the characteristics of the particular desert area without having to grapple closely with navigation and routefinding before striking out cross country.

Trekking Cross Country

Many hikers never leave the trails. That's a shame, because everything that eases your travel through the desert also holds you at a distance. Every hiker knows

that cars and roads keep you out of contact with the land you're traveling through, but many don't realize that trails do the same to a lesser degree. Only by trekking off-trail can you really begin to appreciate the unspoiled desert.

Of course, cross-country hiking is harder than trail hiking. Now all the responsibility for routefinding and navigation falls directly on your shoulders. Not only do you have to find your way to your destination without the help of trail signs but you also have to grapple closely with the details, from deciding whether to stick to a ridge or follow an adjacent wash, to deciding how to avoid a patch of brush.

Paddling the Desert

In some desert areas you can travel by water, strange as it may seem. Rivers traverse the desert on their way from mountains to sea, and some of the best white water in the country is found on desert rivers. There are also calmer desert rivers. The Colorado has the incomparable 260-mile white water run through the Grand Canyon in Arizona, while the Green River has a scenic flat-water stretch in Utah through Canyonlands National Park. Dams have been built in large numbers on desert rivers and streams, and the resulting reservoirs offer some interesting possibilities. Though most of these man-made lakes are frequented by powerboats and are hardly wilderness, some of them offer access to wild country along their shores. Examples are the slickrock canyon country around Lake Powell in southern Utah, and the Verde River in central Arizona, part of which is a designated Wild and Scenic River and flows through the remote Mazatzal Wilderness.

The details of river running and flat-water paddling are beyond the scope of this book.

Opposite: Great Basin petroglyph

Chapter 3

Water and Climate

Desert travelers who venture away from cities and paved roads must pay attention to their water supply. You need water to function. A human without water can survive only about two days outside in the desert summer. Even during the cool part of the year, the dry desert air sucks moisture from your body at a far greater rate than in humid regions. As a desert explorer, you must make certain you have enough water, and safeguard your supply against accidental loss. When traveling by vehicle, you can carry all you need, but not so much that you can waste it. On a day hike or bike ride, you must carry enough water to stay hydrated, which can be a big load during hot weather. On an extended backpack trip, you must carry enough water to reach the next desert water source, as well as to retreat to the last water source if one turns out to be dry. Failure to do so can result in discomfort, serious illness, or death.

How Much Do I Need?

Only experience and your particular technique can tell you how much water you'll need, but I can certainly offer guidelines. An easy walk during cool weather may require only 1 quart per person. The same walk on a summer day with temperatures above 110 degrees F may require 2 or 3 quarts per person. You'll probably find that you'll need 2 or 3 quarts for a long, strenuous hike or bike ride during the cool season. Do the same hike or ride on a hot summer day, and you may guzzle 2 gallons.

Yucca on dune, White Sands National Monument, Chihuahuan Desert

It's easy for me to tell you to err on the safe side and carry more water than you'll need, but it'll be hard for you to do it. I'm reluctant to make myself carry enough water sometimes, even after all my years of desert trekking. On most desert adventures water is the heaviest thing in your pack. On the plus side, if you drink frequently, as you should, your load quickly gets lighter.

Carrying Water in Your Vehicle

Since weight isn't a major consideration, you can use strong containers when you carry your water supply in your car or truck. It's best to use multiple smaller containers for water, rather than one or two large containers. That way, if one container leaks or breaks, you lose just a small portion of your supply. Sometimes I use 1-gallon plastic jugs, the type that drinking water comes in at the supermarket. Although they are lightweight, the plastic is tough. I replace the jugs every season because the plastic ages and gets brittle. A more durable solution is plastic jerry cans, which are available in various capacities from 1 to 10 gallons. Again, it's a good idea to split your water into several smaller jerry cans. I'm not at all a fan of steel jerry cans, especially carried on outside racks. The sun quickly heats the water, which is okay for a hot shower, but not for drinking.

Carrying Water on Foot or Bicycle

For many years, Nalgene bottles have been the standard bottle for hiking and backpacking. The bottles are made in both high-density polyethylene (HDPE) and polycarbonate (PC). Nalgene bottles come in wide and narrow mouths in various sizes. The 1-liter (1 liter = 1.05 quarts) size is by far the most popular. Both HDPE and PC

Cactus blossom

are strong and don't flavor water or drink mixes. The lids are also strong and have a reliable seal. Don't leave plastic water bottles in the sun for hours or days. Sunlight rots most plastics, and eventually it becomes brittle and breaks easily.

The problem with rigid plastic bottles is that they are bulky when you have to carry a lot of water. And the bulk stays in your pack after the water is gone. For years I've searched for the ideal collapsible water bottle, and I think the Platypus line by Cascade Designs comes pretty close. Made of multiple thin layers of laminated plastic, these bottles come in sizes from 0.5 to 2.4 liters and are far more durable than they feel. Eventually, repeated folding does cause cracks, but they generally start in one layer and don't cause leaks. I've never had a leaky bottle as long as I discarded it at the first sign of cracking. The caps seem flimsy, and I have seen one break, so I carry a couple of spares. Push-pull sport tops are also available that make it easy to get a quick drink without removing the cap.

Wide-mouth bottles are easier to use in the field than narrow-mouth bottles. You can fill them much faster and it's easy to add powdered drink mixes. The only thing I don't like about Platypus bottles is that they don't make a wide-mouth version. Nalgene does have a line of collapsible containers with wide mouths.

Hydration systems are the current rage for mountain biking. These consist of a flexible water reservoir, a hose, and a bite valve. The idea is that you can drink without having to stop, take off your pack, and pull out a water bottle. You can buy hydration day packs that have a built-in reservoir, or buy a separate hydration system and use it with an existing pack. Most new day packs and multiday packs have pockets for hydration reservoirs, as well as an opening in the back panel for the hose. Hydration hoses are available for standard Platypus collapsible bottles, so you can use them either way.

Since the hydration hose is exposed to the sun where it runs from your pack over your shoulder, the water warms up quickly. If you're taking frequent drinks this isn't a problem, but at slower rates of consumption the first couple of sips can be hot.

Avoid metal canteens and water bottles. They cause the water to get hot and are not as reliable as high-quality plastic bottles.

Hydration systems are especially prone to leakage. If anything presses on the bite valve, it opens and you can lose the contents of the reservoir in a few minutes. I've taken off my pack, accidentally set it on the bite valve, and had my entire water supply soak into the

> Once, on the first day of an overnight hike to the top of a waterless desert peak, I realized that the water trickling down my leg wasn't sweat—it was coming from the bottom of my pack! After a quick search, I discovered that a water bottle cap was slightly loose. Now, after filling a bottle, collapsible container, or hydration system, I always test for leaks by inverting it and squeezing hard.

ground unnoticed. In keeping with the idea of splitting my water supply among several containers, I generally use a 1-liter Platypus bottle with the hydration hose and refill it from my other bottles as needed. That way, I limit my potential loss to a liter or less.

At present, I carry a Platypus hydration hose on most hikes and rides, though I don't always use it. On day hikes and bike rides, I bring one or two 1-liter Platypus bottles, supplemented by a 2.4-liter Platypus bottle for longer and hotter treks. On backpack trips, I always carry one 1-liter and at least two 2.4-liter Platypus bottles. That way I have enough capacity for a dry camp, even if water sources are plentiful. If I expect to carry a lot of water, I'll take as many as four 2.4-liter Platypus bottles. I keep the 1-liter bottle (with sport cap) handy for my current drinking supply or for use with the hydration hose.

You should clean and dry all water bottles after a trip. I wash wide-mouth Nalgene bottles in the dishwasher. Narrow-mouth bottles, collapsible containers, and hydration reservoirs should be rinsed with vinegar or baking soda and allowed to dry inverted. Store all water containers with the caps off or loose.

Caching Water

In rare cases, such as for hikes on long trails, you may need to cache water in advance. Mice and other rodents have been known to chew through plastic containers, so glass or metal is safest for this type of use. Another option is to use plastic bottles inside a metal box or enclosure. Never place a water cache in the sun. Not only does the sun heat the water but it also rots plastic containers. I once found an old 1 gallon milk jug, still full of water, partially protected from the sun under a small rock overhang. When I touched the jug, the plastic shattered, instantly dumping the water on the ground.

You must hide your cache carefully so that light-fingered people won't steal it, but at the same time note the location carefully so that you can find it again as you pass by, perhaps months later. Ideally, a water cache should be buried, if the soil isn't too rocky. To make certain I can find the cache later on my trip, I mark the location on a map and make notes of the local landmarks and the distance and direction to the cache. You could also mark the location with a GPS receiver, if you have one. Don't rely solely on the GPS—write down the coordinates as well as saving them in the receiver, and also note landmarks in case you arrive later with a broken or dead GPS unit.

Finding Water

An ability to find water separates the experienced desert trekker from the novice. It's a critical skill and a particularly gratifying one to master. Desert water sources include permanent and seasonal streams, springs, wells, rain catchments (guzzlers), seasonal or permanent lakes, ponds and reservoirs, and rock tanks. All these

Getting water from a spring, Paria Canyon, Great Basin Desert

features are marked on USGS topographic maps and are usually shown on land management agency maps as well. That's the good news. The bad news is that desert water information on maps is not reliable. Many sources such as water pockets and rock tanks are seasonal, and even permanent streams, lakes, and springs dry up. Wells and guzzlers may dry up or fail from lack of maintenance. Although you can't rely on water sources shown on maps, they make a good starting point for your search. See Chapter 8 for details on trip planning around water sources and Chapter 9 for information on finding water in an emergency.

Filtering and Purification

All water sources in the field should be treated to remove dangerous organisms before being used for drinking or cooking. Failure to do so risks serious illness. Water can be contaminated by wild animals, domesticated stock, and human activity. Careless human sanitation causes the most dangerous water contamination. Water can also be polluted by chemicals, either artificial or natural. Serious chemical pollution is rare in backcountry areas far from concentrated human activity, but occasionally desert springs are so heavy with dissolved salts that they are undrinkable. Very rarely, springs may actually be poisonous. Springs and pools with no plant or animal life should be regarded with suspicion, except for obviously fresh, temporary water pockets.

It is impossible for you to tell in the field whether backcountry water is contaminated with microscopic life that can cause illness. Even the clearest, freshest desert stream can be dangerous because of a slob camp or animal activity just upstream out of sight. Waterborne illnesses are caused by cysts, protozoa, bacteria, and viruses.

At present, the most popular method of water treatment is a pump microfilter. Microfilters force water through pores that are small enough to trap all organisms except viruses. Since waterborne viral diseases are rare in the North American deserts, such microfiltration produces safe water. Some filters have activated carbon elements as well, which removes some chemical contaminants. All microfilters improve the taste of the water. A few have active iodine elements that kill viruses—such filters are called purifiers because they remove all dangerous organisms. Microfilters have several disadvantages. They are heavy and bulky for backpacking purposes, and the filter elements tend to clog, especially in silty water. Look for a filter system that has a prefilter that removes silt and other visible contaminants before they reach the microfilter. The microfilter should be replaceable or field cleanable. Filters are also slow—an important factor to consider for large groups that require a lot of water.

Water can be purified with several different chemical treatments. Iodine water-purification tablets are easy to use and kill all dangerous organisms (including viruses) except cryptosporidium. Iodine tablets take 30 minutes to purify a quart of

Filtering water with a modified coffee-filter holder. Iodine purification tablets from the small bottle will be added afterward.

water, and of course many quarts can be treated simultaneously. Iodine does leave an aftertaste that some people don't like. Some iodine tablets come with iodine remover tablets, which improve the taste. Fruit-drink mixes containing ascorbic acid (vitamin C) do the same thing. In either case, wait 30 minutes for the iodine to purify the water before adding remover tablets or fruit-drink mixes. I prefer iodine, and neither I nor any member of my party has ever become sick from contaminated water while using it. Make certain you follow the directions carefully, and don't overlook any of your containers as you fill them. I once had two members of my party get sick during the night after drinking from a water bottle that had not been treated. Luckily both were fine in the morning and were able to continue the hike.

Chlorine-dioxide tablets kill all dangerous organisms, including cryptosporidium, but they are expensive and take 4 hours to work.

Both types of halogen tablets lose their purifying qualities if exposed to water or damp air. Keep the bottle tightly closed between uses. I always start a trip with fresh, sealed bottles.

You can also boil water to purify it. Bringing water to a rolling boil at any altitude kills all disease organisms, but it takes time and fuel. Also, because boiling drives out dissolved air, boiled water tastes flat. You can improve the taste by pouring the water between two containers to replace the air.

Neither boiling nor chemical treatments do anything to remove visible matter, such as silt or bits of vegetation. Paper coffee filters, used with a plastic filter holder, make an effective and very light filter system. Such prefiltering also improves the effectiveness of chemical treatments by removing organic matter that binds up the chemical agent.

Opposite: Desert creeks create lush riparian zones, Sycamore Creek, Sonoran Desert.

Climate and Elevation

Next to the availability of water, climate and elevation ranks second in trip planning. The deserts feature a great range of climates. By choosing the best season, you can enjoy the desert at its best. People new to desert exploration often overlook the effect of elevation on desert climate. Generally speaking, higher elevations have cooler, wetter weather. When the desert valleys are roasting hot in late spring, you can still find cool hiking weather along the highest ridges. On the other hand, if the mountains are being pounded by snowstorms in the middle of winter, you can usually escape to the lowest desert valleys and ranges and enjoy dry and sunny weather.

Seasons

The sweeping statement that the desert has only two seasons, hot and not so hot, is only partially true. But there are definitely times of the year when the desert is at its most inviting, and times when it's better to be at the seaside or high in the mountains.

Summer

Summer is the serious season in the desert. Temperatures are at their hottest and all those who can, both animal and human, have flown to cooler climates or hunkered down in cool burrows and air-conditioned buildings. Because temperatures routinely top 110 degrees F in the Sonoran and Mojave Deserts (the North American record is 134 degrees F in Death Valley) and the sun glares down harshly from nearly overhead, only those who must venture out in midday. Humans who work or play outside during the summer are at risk of dehydration, heat exhaustion, severe sunburn, and heatstroke. All but the most die-hard desert explorers either avoid the summer or confine themselves to the highest desert areas, such as the mountains in the Great Basin Desert. Those who do venture into the hot desert backcountry need to be especially prepared to deal with the extreme heat. Late summer brings the threat of thunderstorms to the Sonoran Desert, where storms

Thunderstorms can form quickly over the desert.

typically form over the mountains during the afternoon and move over the desert in the evening. These storms often produce brief heavy rain, which can send floods raging down normally dry washes. Another summer hazard is sudden dust storms, which are especially common in areas where the desert soil has been disturbed by current or former agriculture. Dust storms can abruptly reduce visibility to 0.25 mile or less, and frequently cause serious multiple car accidents on desert highways.

Autumn

Fall is the prime season in the Great Basin and Chihuahuan Deserts and the higher portions of the Sonoran and Mojave Deserts. The extreme temperatures of summer moderate by October, yet nights remain well above freezing. There's little risk of rain storms, and serious windstorms are rare.

Winter

The best time to explore the lowest desert areas, primarily in the Mojave and Sonoran Deserts, is winter. Except on the highest peaks, snowfall is rare and doesn't linger on the ground. Although nighttime temperatures can drop below freezing, most winter nights are moderate and the daytime temperatures are delightful. Winter storms can bring periods of gentle rain, but these short events are separated by days of clear skies and sunny weather. Desert mountains are the earliest to benefit from winter rain, as water pockets fill and grass appears. You'll find great variability from year to year, but if the winter proves to be a wet one, streams start to flow in some of the mountains and, at least for a while, you don't have to think about water all the time. And during this time the foundation may be laid for the desert's famous spring flower show.

Spring

Early spring weather is still reasonably cool in the lower portions of the Mojave and Sonoran. By late spring these areas start to get warm as daytime highs reach the 90s F. Increasing heat and sunlight warms the desert soil, where trillions of seeds lie in wait. If conditions are just right—enough winter and early spring rain at the right times—flowers appear over vast areas. Flowering starts as early as January in the lowest portions of the Mojave and Sonoran Deserts in southwestern Arizona and southeastern California, and it can continue well into May at higher elevations. Desert flowers bloom every year, but the best years have to be seen to be believed. Entire hillsides and valley floors can be covered by golden Mexican poppy. The desert positively reeks of flowers, buzzes with insects, and hums with hummingbirds taking advantage of the sudden bounty. In April and May the cactus put forth their blossoms, the largest and most colorful of all.

The same rainfall that triggers the spring flower show also fills water pockets and replenishes the shallow groundwater that feeds springs and streams, easing the water burdens of desert trekkers.

If there's a downside to spring in the desert, it's the wind. Especially in the Great Basin Desert, spring windstorms are frequent, as the winter storm track moves north and the southern fringe of cold fronts brush the Southwest. Your windshield can be sandblasted into frosted glass in a matter of hours if you attempt to drive in such a storm.

Weather

You probably don't want to set off on a desert trip just as the heaviest rains of the millennium move in. Trying to walk across a complex of sand dunes during a windstorm is also undesirable. It's a good idea, therefore, to check the weather carefully before your trip. Look at recent actual weather as well as the forecast. If the weather has been dry at your destination for several months, you can expect that water pockets, tanks, and seasonal springs will be dry. Recent heavy rains may

Opposite: Spring wildflowers, Big Horn Mountains, Sonoran Desert

A developed desert spring, covered and piped to a watering trough

have filled tanks and pockets but could have also washed out your approach road. Check the forecast carefully, but also remember that it's an educated guess and becomes less reliable further in the future. Don't let a forecast for benign weather fool you into taking too little clothing and shelter.

Chapter 4

Desert Hazards

lthough deserts have their own unique hazards, they aren't inherently dangerous. Knowledge and experience are the keys to having a safe and enjoyable desert trek or drive.

The Plants Are Out to Get You

When most people think of desert, they think of cactus. It's true that cactus spines are a hazard, but there are other spiny plants to watch for, as well as poisonous plants.

Cactus

When I first started hiking in the desert, my older friends warned me about jumping cholla. It seemed this cactus would lie in wait for unsuspecting hikers and hurl sharp spines at the hapless victim. Fearfully, I edged between clumps of this cactus, trying to stay as far away as possible. Some friends. I later learned that jumping cholla can't jump at all and that its name isn't even jumping cholla; it's teddy bear cholla. Its reputation probably comes from the fact that this cactus of the Sonoran Desert looks cuddly. Fuzzy-looking light yellow branches and stems make up the bulk of the plant, which grows about 3 or 4 feet high. Look closely (but not *too* closely) and you'll see that the fuzz is actually thousands of slender, razor-sharp spines. And here's the real secret—each of these spines is covered with microscopic barbs, just like those on a fishhook, only a lot smaller. As the cactus

Soft and fuzzy-looking teddy bear cholla is actually covered with thousands of needle-sharp barbed spines.

grows, the tips of the branches, called joints, separate from the plant and hang loosely before falling off to become cholla burrs. If an animal or human brushes one of these joints, even lightly, the barbed spines grab and don't let go. The victim inevitably takes the joint along for a ride before getting rid of it. If the joint lands in a favorable place, a new plant will germinate. The hazard to hikers (and mountain-bike riders and air-filled sleeping pads) is not the standing plants, which are easily avoided. It's the burrs that litter the ground around the cactus. These little balls of barbs weather gradually from their initial shade of light, golden yellow to desert brown and gray that blends in perfectly with the desert surface. It's all too easy to pick up a cholla burr on your foot and then transfer it to your calf or some other part of your anatomy—usually painfully. Dogs are especially good at this. Burrs that are only lightly attached are easy to remove by inserting a comb under the burr and then carefully flicking it away from you and any morbidly curious bystanders. A burr that is more seriously embedded (you sat on one, or your dog got a bad case) may require pliers to remove the deeply embedded spines.

Other species of cholla, such as chain fruit and Christmas tree cholla, like to litter the ground with small clusters of nearly invisible spines. These specialize in puncturing air mattresses and self-inflating pads. Other cactus to watch out for include several species of pincushions. These plants grow in small clusters, often just a few inches across, and blend into the desert ground. Their tiny spines are just as efficient as cholla at puncturing air mattresses. See the "Camping" section in Chapter 8 for more on this.

Avoiding cactus is pretty easy. Just watch where you place your hands and feet. As you gain experience, you'll find that you are avoiding cactus plants, burrs, and loose spines without really thinking about it. I once took a new acquaintance up a desert rock climb. Afterward he said he liked the route except for the little cactuses he kept getting into. At first I thought, "What cactus?", but then I looked around and noticed the little pincushion cactus on the ledges and in the cracks. To the eye, these 1- or 2-inch-high fuzzy cactus balls looked just like the tufts of yellow grass that also grew on the rock. My friend had constantly been getting his fingers into the pincushions as he looked for holds, but I had enough experience to subconsciously avoid them.

Not all spine-toting desert plants are members of the cactus family. Agave, a

Agave. This plant does not make a good seat!

member of the lily family, has a series of daggerlike leaves growing outward from the base. Each thick, stiff leaf has a series of large, curved barbs growing along the edges and is tipped with a very sharp spine. These can do serious damage if you fall on one. You'll want to be especially careful when edging past agaves on steep or loose terrain.

Poison Ivy

You may encounter poison ivy in moist canyon bottoms and drainages at intermediate elevations in the desert. The leaves and stems of the low-growing plant contain an organic acid that causes a skin reaction in many people. Prevention is the best cure—learn to recognize the plant by its glossy leaves that grow in groups of three and by recognizing the places where you can expect to see it. Poison ivy can be expected when there's flowing water, but it also grows without nearby surface water. It's usually associated with five-leaved wild grape, which is more common. So when you're blasting down that easy canyon bottom and wild grape appears, keep a wary eye out for its poisonous neighbor. Remember that the acid in the sap can adhere to walking sticks, boots, clothing, and dogs, so be careful handling any of these items if you suspect a previous encounter with poison ivy. Wash your clothing promptly after any trek through poison ivy—and wash the dog also. Soap and water removes the acid from human skin, so if you even suspect you've brushed the plants, wash thoroughly as soon as possible after the exposure to minimize the reaction. Even plain water is effective. Calamine lotion relieves the itching and lowers the chance of spreading the reaction by scratching the blisters. In severe cases, you may need to seek medical attention.

> I said that poison ivy is low-growing, but once, in a side canyon off Dark Canyon in Utah, I found myself nervously edging past 6-foot-tall poison ivy plants. There was just a narrow space between the giant plants and the rock wall, and the side canyon was my only way out of Dark Canyon. I needed to return to the car that day, so I turned sideways and moved carefully. As my pack scraped the wall, the shiny leaves were only a few inches from my nose.

Animals that Slither and Skulk by Night

Many would-be desert adventurers are put off by the desert's wild animals, but there's no need to worry unduly. All of the desert's animal life is focused on life and survival, not on attacking people. Understanding how these desert denizens go about their lives is key to avoiding the small hazard they present to us.

Snakes

North American deserts are home to many species of snakes, some poisonous, most not. The two most common rattlesnakes are the Western Diamondback and the Mojave. Western Diamondbacks are the largest desert rattlesnakes and may reach 7 feet in length. They are found throughout the Southwestern deserts, tending to favor lower country. The Mojave rattlesnake is smaller but has more dangerous venom, and ranges from low desert to rocky mountain ridges. I've seen Mojaves as high as 8,000 feet in ponderosa pine forest. Rattlesnakes have been reported as high as 11,000 feet in the western United States.

Rattlesnakes strike fear into the hearts of many novice hikers, but there's no need to let fear of rattlesnakes ruin your enjoyment of the desert. As with other outdoor

Rattlesnake in the trail, early morning, Four Peaks Wilderness, Sonoran Desert

hazards, knowledge and common sense can greatly reduce the danger. Hikers and outdoor recreationists are rarely bitten—most rattlesnake bites happen to people working around places such as woodpiles, where rattlesnakes tend to hide, or when someone attempts to handle or catch a snake. It's important to know that rattlesnakes are probably more frightened of you than you are of them. You'll never see most of the snakes that you pass, because they sense you first and move quietly away. Only if surprised or cornered will a rattlesnake rattle. When you hear this unmistakable sound, stop where you are and locate the snake before moving away. I once was startled by a loud rattle as I walked up a trail in Arizona's Mazatzal Mountains. After listening for a moment, I thought the snake was about 30 feet away, so I started to move farther along the brushy trail. After a couple of steps, I spotted the snake only about 10 feet up the trail. That was a lesson I've never forgotten; always locate the snake visually before moving. I backed off and circled the snake through the brush, staying about 20 feet away in case it decided to move.

Rattlesnakes prey on mice and other small rodents and don't deliberately attack humans. It's possible that surprised snakes might move toward you at first, but normally their senses tell them right where you are. You need to return the favor and keep an eye out for them. As you walk, watch the ground about 10 to 20 feet in front of you. If you want to look at the scenery, stop first. Keep an especially sharp eye on hidden spots, such as deep shade under rocks and bushes. Rattlesnakes can strike about one half their body length, and most rattlesnakes are 4 feet long or less. So don't walk or place a hand or foot within several feet of blind spots. Go around or step up on large rocks or logs and see what's on the far side before stepping down.

I was cruising down a desert creek late one afternoon, nearly back at the car after a rough and tiring cross-country hike. I was pretty much lost in a reverie, listening to the tinkle of the tiny creek and enjoying the easier walking at the end of the hike. I stepped up on a 3-foot-high boulder that was blocking the way, and was just about to start down the far side when I spotted a coiled rattlesnake at the base of the boulder. The snake never rattled or moved as I stepped off the boulder the way I came and moved carefully around it.

As with other reptiles, rattlesnakes are cold blooded, meaning that they depend on their environment to maintain their body temperature. During the winter, rattlesnakes hibernate in burrows to avoid the cold temperatures, though they may come out temporarily during warm spells. A good rule of thumb is that if lizards are active, rattlesnakes are probably active. Rattlesnakes constantly seek ground that is neither too cold nor too hot. The ideal temperature seems to be about 80 degrees F. This means you should watch for rattlesnakes sunning themselves on open ground when the air is cool. If the temperature is on the hot side, keep an eye out for snakes under shady ledges and bushes. When walking cross-country, stick to open ground as much as possible, which is easy enough in most deserts. When resting, rattlesnakes often coil tightly and half bury themselves in sand. Watch for this distinct shape and learn to avoid it. A friend once stepped right over a coiled, half-buried snake without seeing it. Walking behind, I saw it just before I stepped in the same place.

During the summer, when daytime temperatures are too hot for them, rattlesnakes become nocturnal. Always use a flashlight or headlamp when walking around camp or along a trail at night in warm weather. Other poisonous desert creatures such as scorpions are nocturnal during hot weather as well, so you might want to use a net tent or sleep off the ground.

Rattlesnakes hunt their rodent prey and avoid predators by smell, and by sensing ground and air vibrations. Rattlesnakes also have a pair of small pits between the eyes and above the nose that sense infrared heat, which is why they are known as pit vipers. Apparently they direct their strike at least partially by the infrared heat coming from the body of the victim. Rattlesnake venom paralyzes prey and begins the digestive process. When the snake strikes, at a speed comparable to a trained boxer's punch, it unfolds hollow fangs from the roof of its mouth and punctures the skin of its victim. The venom is injected through the hollow fangs deep into the puncture wound. Small rodents are paralyzed in a few minutes, and the venom literally starts to digest the victim. The snake then swallows its prey whole.

Rattlesnake bites are a serious medical emergency but generally not life threatening. (In Arizona, scorpion stings kill many more people, and Africanized bees have the potential to be more dangerous than scorpions. To put this all in perspective, a few people a year die from such bites, but thousands die in car accidents.) The amount of venom injected varies; purely defensive bites are often dry. Hunting rattlesnakes tend to inject the most venom. Symptoms of a rattlesnake bite vary, but it's generally agreed that severe symptoms indicate that more venom was injected. The first sign is the bite itself, which will have two fang punctures in addition to the bite marks from the snake's upper and lower teeth. The bite will be painful, and swelling and discoloration will spread up the bitten limb. Weakness, trouble breathing, and nausea may also occur. The main dangers are tissue destruction around the site of the bite and infection caused by the deep puncture wounds left by the fangs. Rattlesnake bite victims should be kept calm and transported to a hospital as soon as possible. Identify the snake if possible, but don't risk further injury. The only effective treatment is rattlesnake antivenin, which must be administered under a doctor's care because of possible severe side effects. All of the field treatments that have been proposed over the years, including tourniquets, cutting and sucking, and application of cold packs, have been shown to cause more harm than good.

Never kill or harass rattlesnakes, except around permanent dwellings. As I mentioned above, most victims of snake bite were attempting to handle the snake. Also consider that you'll mostly only see snakes that rattle at you and give you fair warning. If people kill these snakes, they're favoring the evolution of nonrattling rattlesnakes—not a pleasant thought.

Sonoran coral snakes are found in the Sonoran Desert, ranging into southern Arizona. Their venom is more dangerous than that of rattlesnakes, but the snake is so small that it could probably only bite a finger. You'll be lucky if you ever see one. Sonoran coral snakes are marked with bright yellow or cream, red, and black bands, and the colored bands completely encircle the snake. There are several nonpoisonous snakes that have similar colors but the bands do not encircle the snake's body.

A pit viper like the rattlesnake, the copperhead has venom that is similar in potency to the rattlesnake. Unlike rattlesnakes, copperheads do not have rattles. They are found in the northeastern portion of the Chihuahuan Desert, West Texas, and northern Mexico.

Other Reptiles

The only other poisonous reptile in the North American deserts is the Gila monster, found primarily in the saguaro forests of the Sonoran Desert. This large lizard, with distinctive black, orange, pink, and yellow coloring, grows to about 18 inches, including its thick tail. Gila monsters have a neurotoxic venom but no

A rare daylight sighting of a Gila monster

fangs. Instead the venom is secreted around their grooved molars. They grind the venom into their victim with their powerful jaws. Gila monsters appear to be torpid and slow moving but react very quickly when disturbed. Once attached, they inflict a very painful bite and are hard to dislodge. Gila monsters are rare and are protected by Arizona state law. Though very rarely fatal, Gila monster bites are a medical emergency.

Spiders

Dangerous spiders include the black widow and the brown recluse. Both spiders prefer dark, hidden corners. The female black widow (the male is not venomous) is about 1 inch long and can be recognized by the hourglass-shaped red mark on the underside of its abdomen. Although the bite is not very painful, black widow venom is neurotoxic and can be life threatening to small children, the elderly, and those with preexisting health problems, though fatal cases are rare. Symptoms come on rapidly and include a feeling of apprehension, sweating, congestion of the eyes and face, muscular cramps, and pain in the lower body and legs. The victim should be transported to medical care as soon as possible, where antivenin can be administered. Black widow spiders are more likely to be encountered around man-made structures than in the open desert.

Brown recluse spiders have a small, violin-shaped mark on their upper body. The bite is not life threatening, though it does result in an ulcerating wound that is difficult to heal. Medical care should be sought. As with the black widow, brown recluse spiders are found mostly around human structures.

Tarantulas

These large, hairy spiders look fierce and grow to 6 or 7 inches, but they rarely bite humans unless aggravated. Even then, their venom is no worse than a bee or wasp sting. Tarantulas are most commonly seen crossing desert roads on summer nights.

Scorpions

Scorpions have been responsible for more deaths in the North American Desert than any reptile. There are upwards of 800 species of scorpions in the world, all having venom. Most scorpion stings are no worse than that of a yellow jacket, but there is one species that can be lethal. This scorpion, *Centruroides sculpturatus,* is found in southern California, Arizona, southwest New Mexico, Mexico, and Baja California. Smaller than many of the nonlethal scorpions, it is greenish yellow to straw-colored and averages about 2 inches in length. Its behavior also helps identify it. It prefers to cling upside down and is commonly found clinging to the underside of rocks and loose bark. Most of the nonlethal scorpions, while they do hide under rocks and logs, stay upright on the ground. Nonlethal scorpions produce a painful sting with swelling and discoloration at the site. A sting from *C. sculpturatus* causes immediate severe pain but no swelling or discoloration at the site. The sting site becomes hypersensitive. The venom, a neurotoxin, begins to affect the nervous system. Numbness travels up the arm or leg from the sting site. The victim's throat feels tight and the tongue has a thick feeling. The victim may drool, have a fever, and have difficulty breathing. Restlessness occurs and sometimes leads to convulsions. Any sting from *C. sculpturatus* is a medical emergency. Luckily, antivenin is available.

A few simple practices can greatly reduce the danger from scorpions. The primary one is the age-old desert rule of never putting your hands or feet in places you can't see. When picking up rocks, sticks, bark, or logs, kick them over with your shod foot before picking them up. Shake out any footwear, socks, clothing, and other gear that's been on the ground or where scorpions could reach it. Keep your sleeping bag stuffed until you intend to use it, or keep it in a closed tent.

Centipedes

These many-legged creatures grow as long as 8 inches in the American deserts. They look fearsome, and do have a pair of poisonous claws, but their venom is only dangerous to the insects that are their prey. Their legs are sharp-tipped and might scratch you as they run across bare skin—and it would certainly be startling. Centipedes are primarily active at night during the summer. I've seen two—one was on

Centipede, a creature of the Sonoran Desert that looks more dangerous than it is

the inside wall of an old rancher's line cabin, and the other was on my groundsheet, under my air mattress. I've had very few problems with small creatures getting onto my groundsheet, but normally I use slippery plastic that they don't seem to be able to grip. On this occasion I was trying a rough-surfaced type of plastic, hoping I wouldn't slip around as much in my sleeping bag. Apparently the centipede found it agreeable as well. It didn't move when I lifted my air mattress away, but as soon as I pulled an edge of the groundsheet, it shot away with surprising speed into a nearby bush.

Cone-Nosed Bugs

Also known as assassin bugs or kissing bugs, cone-nosed bugs are 0.5 to 1 inch in length and have a cone-shaped head. They feed on the blood of mammals, primarily rodents, but certainly will feast on humans if they have a chance. Cone-nosed bugs are nocturnal and most humans are bitten at night. The bite itself isn't painful, but after a few hours or a day, a hard, itchy welt develops around the site. A few people develop swelling of the arm or leg that was bitten and even experience systemic reactions, such as nausea and increased pulse and respiration rates.

Mosquitoes

Mosquitoes are rare in the desert because of the dryness, but they can some-times be pretty annoying after a rainy period in late winter or early spring. In addition, West Nile disease is carried by mosquitoes and can be passed to humans. Carry insect repellent at all times, and a net tent is not a bad idea after a rainy period. Desert mosquitoes are most active at dusk and at night.

Bees

Bees, especially the exotic Africanized honeybees, are arguably the most dangerous creatures in the American deserts, because many people are allergic to their stings. People who are allergic should consult their doctor and carry a bee-sting kit with them.

Africanized honeybees were accidentally released into the wild in South America during the 1960s and have since spread northward into all the North American deserts except the Great Basin. Africanized bees freely interbreed with European honeybees, and the two are difficult to tell apart in the field. Because of their aggressive behavior, Africanized bees are also called "killer" bees. While their venom is no more potent than that of the ordinary European honeybee, Africanized bees are more aggressive at defending their hive and swarms.

Although most encounters with Africanized bees occur in and around cities and towns, you should take a few precautions while exploring the desert. Avoid all concentrations of bees—especially hives and swarms. Domestic hives should be avoided also, because not all beekeepers keep their hives free of Africanized bees. If attacked, drop your pack and run. Protect your eyes and don't swat at the bees; apparently the smell of crushed bees makes the survivors more aggressive. Take shelter in a tent, vehicle, or building, if available. A beekeeping friend advises that all bees are confused by dense foliage or brush. Jumping into water is reported not to be effective, because Africanized bees wait for the victim to reappear. On the other hand, Africanized bees don't chase for more than about 0.5 mile, so a healthy person should be able to outrun them. In fact, nearly all the human fatalities have been the very young, the elderly, and other people unable to escape.

Predators

Bobcats, coyotes, mountain lions, and other predators are not usually a threat to humans. Mexican gray wolves have been reintroduced to the Mogollon Moun-tains in New Mexico and the Blue River country in Arizona, and may possibly spread to adjacent desert areas, but they aren't a threat to humans.

Bobcats and coyotes don't bother people. There have been a few cases of mountain lions attacking mountain bikers and runners. People moving fast appear to occasionally look like prey to mountain lions. Normally, lions stalk and kill deer. You'll be extremely lucky to even see a mountain lion in the wild—I've only seen tracks. If you do become aware that you are being stalked, experts advise you to stand your ground and make yourself look as large and formidable as possible. Stand up, spread your jacket wide, but don't make eye contact with the cat. If attacked, fight back with your pocketknife or anything at hand.

If you see any animal behaving strangely—nocturnal animals wandering around in daylight or losing their normal fear of people—suspect rabies. Rabies outbreaks occasionally occur in wild animal populations, especially those near towns and cities. The possibility of being bitten by a rabid animal is another good reason to avoid feeding or handling wildlife.

Old Mines

The desert has always attracted prospectors because of its open character and widespread rock outcrops. Some desert mountain ranges are literally honeycombed with mine shafts and tunnels, and nearly all show some signs of past mining activity. Mine shafts and tunnels are unstable and extremely dangerous. Besides the obvious dangers of cave-ins and unexpected vertical shafts, mines also tend to collect poisonous or

Abandoned mine shafts are common in the desert but are not always marked.

radioactive gases. Abandoned mine shafts are supposed to be sealed or barricaded, but in practice many are not. Vertical shafts and prospect holes are especially dangerous in brushy country and at night.

Floods

At first glance, flooding may seem to be an unlikely desert hazard, but look again. Most desert topography is shaped by water and flooding. The evidence is everywhere, in dry washes spreading from the foot of desert mountain ranges, and in logs jammed between the walls of narrow canyons, dozens of feet above the bed. Both steady winter rains and sudden summer thunderstorms can produce flooding. Winter rains tend to be light but persistent. At first, the thirsty desert soil soaks up the rain, but if the rainfall continues for several days, the ground becomes saturated and runoff may increase rapidly. Rain falling on the highest mountains also melts what snow may have accumulated. Creeks and riverbeds that have been dry for years may carry large volumes of water, sometimes for weeks on end.

Violent summer thunderstorms can cause flash floods miles from the storm. Heavy rain falling on bare desert soil or rock runs off much faster than it can be absorbed, and it quickly collects in tributary drainages. As the drainages combine, the flood gathers force and volume, and often takes the form of a wall of water moving down a dry wash. Because of the carrying capacity of fast-moving water, flash floods usually contain a large amount of soil, sand, gravel, and even boulders. Rapid erosion of the stream bed takes place, and paved roads and stream crossings can be destroyed in minutes. Never try to cross a flooded wash on foot or in a vehicle. The roadbed may be gone and the water is usually deeper than you expect. Just 1 foot of fast-moving water is enough to wash away a vehicle.

Never park a vehicle or camp in a dry wash. Despite repeated warnings, every year vehicles are washed away and people lose their lives in desert washes.

Heat Hazards

Summer is the serious season in the desert. Those adventurers who explore the desert during the hottest time of the year must be prepared and experienced. Even during the fall, winter, and spring, the air is often dry and warm and heat injury is a possibility.

Dehydration

Two thirds of the body's weight is water. Dehydration occurs when not enough water is consumed to make up for the water used by the body for metabolism, elimination, and sweating. The body uses anywhere from a cup of water per hour in cool, resting conditions to a quart per hour or more during strenuous activity in hot weather. You can stay hydrated by regulating how much your body uses and by consuming enough water to make up for the loss.

Since water consumption goes up rapidly with an increase in heat and strenuous activity, it makes sense to curtail your activities during the hottest part of the day. (See Chapter 8 for practical tips.)

Sweating is the body's mechanism for keeping cool under heat stress. In a humid environment, sweating is obvious as moisture collects on the skin. In an arid environment, such as the desert, skin moisture evaporates rapidly and a desert trekker can lose significant amounts of moisture insensibly, without sweating. That's why you must be aware of your environment and make sure you consume plenty of water, even if you're not sweating. Mild dehydration impairs body function, while severe dehydration results in death. Symptoms of progressively worse dehydration are thirst, discomfort, loss of appetite, flushed skin, impatience, increased pulse rate, elevated body temperature, sleepiness, nausea, dizziness, headache, difficulty in breathing, tingling in the limbs, loss of salivation, bluish skin, indistinct speech, loss of ability to walk, delirium, spastic movements, swollen tongue and inability to swallow, deafness, dim vision, painful urination, shriveled and numb skin, and death. Dehydration is clearly not a nice way to go. Water, of course, is the primary treatment for dehydration, and if the dehydration isn't too serious, recovery is rapid. Serious cases must be moved to a cool environment if possible and transported to medical care as soon as possible.

Heat Exhaustion and Sunstroke

Other heat hazards are heat exhaustion and sunstroke. Heat exhaustion occurs when the body moves excessive amounts of blood from the core to the extremities in an attempt to keep the core at normal temperature. Heat exhaustion victims are weak, pale, sweat profusely, have a weak pulse, breathe rapidly and shallowly, feel dizzy, and may lose consciousness. Treatment consists of moving the victim to as cool a place as possible, providing electrolyte replacement drinks, and aiding the body's cooling efforts by removing as much clothing as possible and providing ventilation to aid the sweating process.

Sunstroke, or heatstroke, occurs when the brain loses control of the body's

Summer Hikes
Telescope Peak, Death Valley
Ruby Crest Trail, Ruby Mountains
Toyaibe Crest Trail, Toyaibe Range
Mount Charleston Loop, Spring Range
Wheeler Peak, Great Basin National Park
Duffey Peak, Pine Forest Range
KP-Grants Creek Loop, Blue Range Primitive Area
Mogollon Crest Trail, Mogollon Mountains

heat regulating system. Sunstroke is a medical emergency and results in death unless promptly treated. Sunstroke comes on suddenly and the primary symptom is hot, dry skin (as opposed to the pale, clammy, sweaty skin of heat exhaustion victims). Other symptoms include full, fast pulse; rapid breathing that later becomes shallow and faint; dilated pupils; early loss of consciousness; involuntary muscle twitching; convulsions; and body temperature of 105 degrees F and higher. The victim must be promptly treated by being moved to a cool location, removing as much clothing as possible, making certain the airway is open, reducing body temperature by wrapping the victim with wet cloths or by dousing with water, and transporting to medical care as soon as possible. If cold packs are available, they should be placed around the neck, under the arms, and at the ankles, where blood vessels lie close to the skin.

> I've only once encountered a case of heat exhaustion, and luckily never a case of sunstroke. A friend and I were rock climbing on a warm spring day, and I didn't think it was all that hot. But, as I found out, susceptibility to heat injury varies among people. Toward the end of the descent from the climb, he began to feel weak and very tired and started to exhibit the classic symptoms. It took him several hours in an air-conditioned house and a lot of cool drinks to recover.

Hypothermia

Hypothermia is a medical emergency caused by the loss of the body's ability to keep warm. No experienced desert explorer would be surprised that hypothermia can occur in the desert. Desert nights are usually cool, and often downright cold, because the dry, clear atmosphere allows the earth to rapidly radiate heat to the dark sky. In addition, the open desert often lacks natural shelter from wind-driven rain. Hypothermia is often thought of as something that only happens in subzero conditions in snow and ice, but actually the most dangerous conditions are the subtle ones—cool but not cold temperatures (40 to 60 degrees F), light wind (5 to 10 mph), and rain or mist. Wind causes heat to be lost from objects in its path much more rapidly than in still air, and most of the effect is in the first few miles per hour of wind. Such wind chill is increased if the victim is wearing wet clothing, which increases heat loss by evaporation, and is aggravated by clothing that loses its insulating ability when wet.

The body produces heat by metabolizing food and water. So the key to preventing hypothermia is to stay hydrated, eat high-energy foods during periods of strenuous exercise, and wear the right amount of protective clothing. It's especially important to choose clothing made of fibers that shed water and retain their insulating ability when wet. (See Chapter 6 for clothing information.)

The early stages of hypothermia can be treated by wrapping the victim in insulating clothing or sleeping bags, and providing warm drinks and food. Once the body's temperature regulating system breaks down, hypothermia becomes a medical emergency just as serious as sunstroke. External heat must be provided, preferably in the form of other people, or in the form of warm water bottles, and the victim must be transported to medical care immediately.

Wind Hazards

Wind contributes to both dehydration and hypothermia, depending on whether it's a hot wind or a cold one. High winds also pick up loose dust and sand and can make it difficult or impossible to travel in the desert.

Dust Storms

Dust storms are common in the North American deserts, and they occur when strong high winds (generally 20 mph or higher) blow across large areas of loose soil and dust. These high winds can be caused by either winter and spring cold fronts or the outflow from summer thunderstorms. Usually, dust-storm-prone areas are those disturbed by human activities, such as agriculture or clearing land for subdivisions. Visibility can suddenly drop to 0.25 mile or less, and travel on foot or bicycle is difficult or impossible. Back-road driving is difficult as well. It's best to seek shelter as soon as possible.

Dust storms striking a highway or freeway are a frequent cause of multiple-car accidents, when drivers abruptly slow down and are rear-ended by oncoming vehicles. The safest action is to get completely off the road and stop. On a highway, turn off into a parking area or secondary road. On a freeway, exit to a rest area or secondary road if possible, or pull completely off the road and turn off your lights. Don't park on the shoulder, and don't leave lights or flashers on. Another vehicle may see your lights and attempt to follow you, not realizing you've stopped.

Dust storms usually abate in a few hours when thunderstorms move on or dissipate, or in the evening when the setting sun causes the wind to drop. Large amounts of dust may linger in the air, obscuring distant landmarks, but visibility is usually more than good enough to continue your desert trip.

Sand Storms

Similar to dust storms, sandstorms occur with winds of 30 mph or greater. Vast areas of open sand are not present in the North American deserts, so wide area sandstorms don't occur. Local sandstorms, in or near sand dunes or disturbed areas, can restrict visibility on freeways and highways. The highly abrasive sand can cause severe damage to vehicles by sandblasting paint and pitting windshields. As with dust storms, get to shelter as soon as you can. Park your vehicle in a garage or carport if available, and seek shelter in a building. In the desert backcountry, look for a steep hill or rock outcrop where you can park and/or camp on the lee side, out of the direct sweep of the wind.

Chapter 5

Navigation

Finding your way in a maze of desert back roads can be quite a challenge. Roads change often in the desert, and maps aren't always updated. Roads that were maintained are abandoned, and new roads are built or created. The edge of civilization, where roads are created rapidly and access points are sometimes blocked, can be especially difficult to navigate. Many desert back roads don't have signs, either. You'll need the best maps you can get, and you should have basic map and compass skills if you plan to explore off the maintained and marked roads. In addition, a Global Positioning System (GPS) receiver can be a great navigation aid in remote areas.

Map Reading for Desert Driving

A map is a diagram representing the features of the landscape such as peaks, rivers, and lakes, and man-made features including trails, roads, buildings, and other structures. All these features are shown by means of various symbols. A legend shows all the symbols used on the map, and explains their meaning. Simple maps may have no legend at all. Detailed maps may not have room on the sheet for a full legend, as is the case with USGS topographic maps. Such maps have a separate symbol sheet or booklet. Bound map atlases usually include a symbol sheet near the front of the atlas. Computer-based maps, such as National Geographic's Topo! series, have the symbols in a help selection on the program's menu. Symbols vary from map to map, depending on the map's purpose. In any case, the first step in map reading is to learn the symbols.

Road maps are almost always planimetric—that is, they show natural and man-made features with symbols but don't show the shape of the land. Topographic maps use contour lines to show elevations and terrain features, such as valleys, canyons, dry washes, ridges, hills, and mountains. Topographic maps can be useful for navigating 4WD roads, since they show the slope of the terrain.

Map Reading for Desert Hiking

Finding your way on a good trail system is largely a matter of reading trail signs. If the signs are accurate and informative, you won't need to refer to your map much at all. Unfortunately, desert trail signs are sometimes misleading or missing.

Topographic Maps

Topographic maps are a must for desert exploration on all but the most well-maintained and signed trail systems. Because topographic maps accurately show the actual shape of the land, which doesn't change much, even older maps are very useful.

Using a map, especially when you're new to map reading, is easier if you first orient the map to the terrain so that north on the map is the same as north on the ground. All good maps are drawn with north up, and a symbol showing north should be printed somewhere on the map. (Beware of any map that is not printed north up—such disregard for cartographic standards means it's not likely to be accurate.) The easiest way to orient a map is to match a prominent landmark in the landscape with the same landmark on the map. Failing such a landmark, you can use your compass to find north.

With experience and practice, topographic maps can give you an immense amount of detail about the terrain and vegetation. Topographic maps use contour lines, usually colored brown, to depict the terrain. Each contour line represents the same elevation all along its length, and the elevation interval between contour lines is printed on the map margin. Maps of flat or gentle terrain have contour intervals of 5, 10, or 20 feet, while maps of steeper, hilly, or mountainous terrain usually have contour lines every 40 or 80 feet. Every fourth or fifth contour line is a major contour line, printed a little darker with the elevation printed along it at intervals. A major contour line with "1800" printed along it, for example, would represent the new coast line if sea level rose 1,800 feet.

Widely spaced contour lines show that the slope is gentle, while closely spaced contour lines tell you that the terrain is steep. Missing contour lines indicate a cliff band. Closely spaced or missing contour lines crossing a canyon bottom mean a dry (or wet) waterfall that may block the canyon. Smoothly curving contour lines probably mean that the slope is fairly even, while jagged contour lines mean rough or rocky terrain. Contour lines forming a V-shape pointing

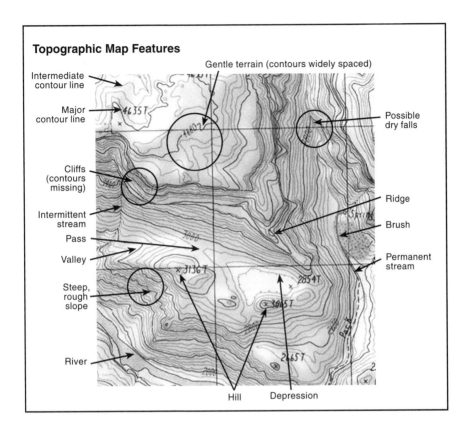

Topographic Map Features

Gentle terrain (contours widely spaced)

Intermediate contour line

Major contour line

Possible dry falls

Cliffs (contours missing)

Ridge

Intermittent stream

Brush

Pass

Valley

Permanent stream

Steep, rough slope

River

Hill   Depression

uphill are depicting a steep-sided valley, canyon, or drainage. If the V shape points downhill, then you're looking at a narrow ridge crest. U-shaped contour lines pointing uphill mean a broader canyon bottom, and likewise, if the U points downhill, the ridge crest is rounded and gentle. Contour lines enclosing an area show a rise, hill, or mountain peak, and circular lines with hatch marks show a crater or depression.

Most topographic maps are shaded with various green symbols to show vegetation. Although general (brush land shown on desert maps can be anything from widely spaced bushes to dense, head-high stands of chaparral), this shading is still useful. For example, if a canyon bottom is shown with brush shading, be prepared for dense brush that may confine you to the stream channel. Remember that desert vegetation is usually thicker on north-facing slopes because of the cooler, moister microclimate. Often, the steeper the slope, the denser the brush—a particularly nasty combination.

Other symbols on a topographic map are usually similar to planimetric maps. When in doubt, consult the map legend or in the case of USGS maps, the free symbol booklet or sheet.

Compass Work

For road navigation, you should carry at least a basic liquid-filled compass to determine north. Avoid cheap compasses. Chances are you won't need your compass all that often, but when you do, you'll need it badly. That is not a good time to find out that it's broken.

Using Your Compass

Compasses have a major gotcha. They don't point north, at least not to true north at the Earth's geographic North Pole. Instead, the magnetized needle aligns itself with the Earth's magnetic field so that the needle points to magnetic north, a point presently in Canada 1,000 miles from the North Pole. Maps are drawn in reference to true north. The difference between true north and magnetic north is called "declination," and it varies from place to place on the Earth's surface. To further complicate things, the magnetic field changes, causing declination to slowly change at any given place. Accurate and precise maps such as the USGS topographic series show the declination and the rate of change per year on the map margin.

Because your compass points to magnetic north, you have to correct it to true north before you can use it to orient your map. Better compasses have a built-in declination adjustment. You can set the declination before a trip to a given area, and then use the compass as a true north instrument. The Silva compass shown in the photo also has a clinometer, which is used for measuring slope angles as well as setting the declination.

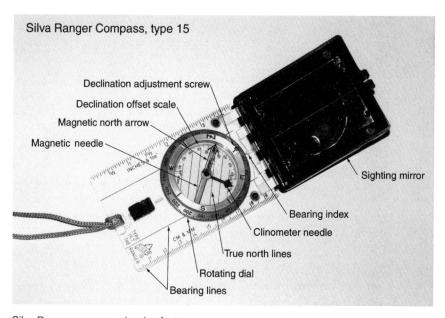

Silva Ranger compass, showing features

For example, in the Sonoran Desert in southern Arizona, the declination is 12 degrees east. That means that the compass needle points 12 degrees east of true north. To convert a magnetic bearing of, say, 80 degrees to the true bearing, you add easterly declination and subtract westerly declination. In this case, 80 degrees magnetic equals 68 degrees true. Do the procedure in reverse to convert true to magnetic. Confused? Just think how tough it is to keep it straight at night, in a storm, when you've lost the trail and need to walk out to the nearest road. I strongly recommend that all desert hikers get a compass with a declination adjustment and then set the adjustment to the local area before the hike. Also, get a compass with a baseplate that can be used to plot bearings on maps. To keep the rest of this section simple, I'm going to assume that you've followed my advice, and I'll refer only to true bearings from now on.

Walking a Compass Bearing

Plotting and walking a bearing lets you go directly to a feature on the map. If there are no serious obstacles such as cliffs or canyons in the way, you can plot a bearing line on the map from your present position to your destination, and then walk the bearing on the ground. To do this, lay the edge of the baseplate, which is your course or bearing line, along the course from your position to the destination. You may need to extend the edge with a straight edge, such as the edge of another map, in order to reach your destination. Then, rotate the compass capsule until its true north arrow is lined up with true north on the map. If your map has a true north grid, so much the better. Lacking one, you can just eyeball the nearest edge

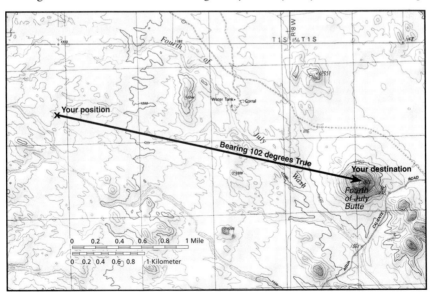

Plotting a bearing

of the map. Don't use UTM grid lines (gray on USGS maps) or public land survey lines (red on USGS maps) because they aren't aligned to true north. The last step is to note the bearing on the azimuth ring on the compass capsule.

Now, put the map away and turn the entire compass until the north end of the needle aligns with the magnetic north reference on the capsule. The compass bearing line is now pointing toward your destination. Note that you didn't actually have to read the bearing, but it's a good idea to note the value in case you accidentally move the compass capsule. Sight along the bearing line, and pick out a landmark on your bearing line that is as far away as possible. Now, all you have to do is walk toward the landmark until you reach your destination. If sight distance is limited because of rolling terrain or hills and you have to pick a fairly close landmark, pick another one beyond it. As you walk, keep the two landmarks aligned. When you reach the first one, pick anther landmark beyond it. This technique keeps you on course even though you can't see very far. You would use this same method if you got the bearing to your destination from a GPS receiver instead of the map.

If obstacles force a detour, you'll still be close to your original course if you are using a distant landmark to navigate by. If you have to use relatively close landmarks, you'll end up offset from your course, but unless you are forced to deviate a long way in one direction, detours tend to cancel themselves out.

Triangulation

If you're uncertain of your position and can see at least two, or preferably three, distinctive landmarks that you can positively identify on the map, you can use map and compass to determine your location. Mountain peaks, buttes, and the edge of a mesa are all good examples of such landmarks. Using your compass, sight on the first landmark and get the bearing, then place your compass on the map and align the rotating capsule's true north indicator with true north on the map. Keep the compass aligned with true north and move it until an edge of the baseplate lies over your landmark. Now draw a line along that edge of the baseplate. Repeat this procedure with your remaining landmarks so that the bearing lines converge and cross. If you have at least three landmarks, you'll see that the three bearing lines don't cross at exactly the same point; instead, they form a (hopefully) small triangle. This "error triangle" is your approximate position. Using just two landmarks is a bad idea because you don't have any means of cross-checking your bearings.

A slightly different version of triangulation can be used when you are on a known linear feature, such as a trail, drainage, or ridge crest. Then you need just two landmarks and bearing lines to determine your location.

Walking to a Baseline

Before entering the backcountry, whether you plan to walk on trails or travel cross-country, you should pick a baseline. This is an unmistakable linear feature, such as a

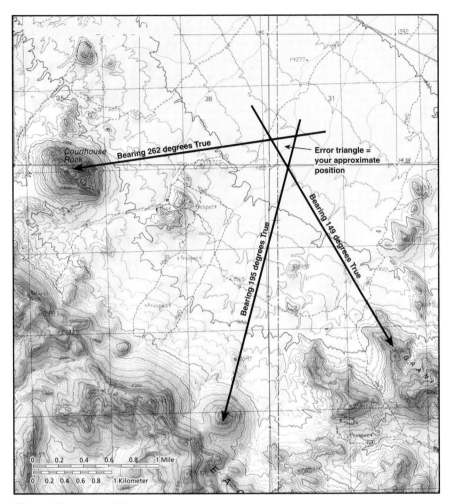

Bearing 262 degrees True

Courthouse Rock

Error triangle = your approximate position

Bearing 149 degrees True

Bearing 195 degrees True

| 0 | 0.2 | 0.4 | 0.6 | 0.8 | 1 Mile |
| 0 | 0.2 | 0.4 | 0.6 | 0.8 | 1 Kilometer |

Triangulating your position

road or well-used trail, that forms one edge of the area you plan to be in. If you get hopelessly lost, you can always walk to your baseline using a compass bearing or, in a pinch, by just walking in the general direction. In either case, you'll eventually reach your baseline and can then follow it to a known point. Of course, you'll probably have to walk a long distance out of your way, so walking to a baseline is always a last resort.

Satellite Assistance for Driving

The Navstar System, usually known as the Global Positioning System, or GPS, has revolutionized land, sea, and air navigation. The technique of GPS land navigation fills entire books, and I refer you to some of those books in the Recommended Reading list if you want to learn more. Here, I'll discuss the basic techniques that are useful for navigation in the desert backcountry.

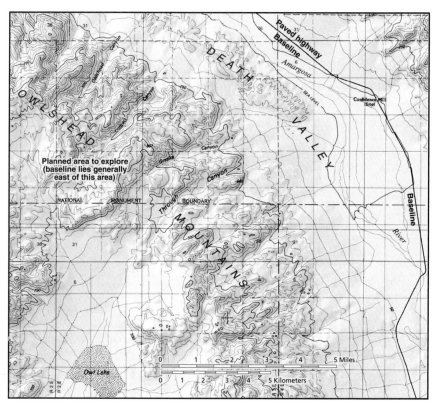

Using a baseline

A GPS receiver computes your position and altitude by receiving signals from four or more GPS satellites. Twenty-one operational satellites placed in intersecting orbits at an altitude of 12,000 miles cover the entire Earth 24 hours per day. The system is operated by the U.S. Department of Defense and is free and open for public use. GPS is not affected by weather or time of day, although the receiver must have a clear view of the sky. Narrow canyons can prevent a GPS receiver from receiving enough satellites, and some of the desert areas are near military test ranges where GPS may be jammed for training exercises. In addition, the receiver can fail or the batteries run down, so GPS should be used to supplement traditional map and compass techniques.

A variety of lightweight, handheld GPS receivers are available that can determine your position to within 30 feet and your altitude to within 100 feet, or better. For extended vehicle use, you'll want to get a receiver with provision for an external roof-mounted antenna, a vehicle mount, and a 12-volt power cable. In all cases, avoid the cheapest receivers, because these often use the older scanning receiver technology, which is not as reliable as the newer parallel channel designs. In practice, I've found that parallel channel receivers can usually see enough of the sky to maintain navigation if placed on the dashboard. High-end receivers have differential receivers (DGPS) for increased accuracy, and moving map displays that can be updated with maps from computer CD-ROMs. DGPS uses supplemental signals from government transmitters placed on known, surveyed points to correct for errors caused by the atmosphere and other factors. DGPS is used primarily for sea and air navigation and by surveyors. For backcountry use, standard GPS is as accurate as the best maps, and you don't really benefit from DGPS.

Moving maps can be useful for highway navigation, and as the maps become more detailed, they will become useful on back roads and even trails. The small size of the display is a limitation, but you can overcome that by using GPS with a laptop computer and a computer-based topographic map program. With such a setup, you can monitor your position in real time on accurate and detailed maps. For recreational purposes, it's probably overkill. However, computer-based maps are very useful for planning a trip at home and setting up your GPS receiver in advance.

Without a map, the position information given by a GPS receiver is useless. GPS receivers display your position, or fix, as a pair of coordinates. To be useful, you must plot the coordinates on a map. Any map accurate enough for use with GPS will have a coordinate system marked on the margins. There are many coordinate systems in use, but the two most common on maps of the North American deserts are latitude and longitude (lat/long) and Universal Transverse Mercator (UTM). Of the two, UTM is the easiest to use in the field, and lat/long is generally only used when the map doesn't have UTM coordinates.

When a cartographer creates a map, he or she uses ground locations, or benchmarks, that have been precisely surveyed and located in relation to other benchmarks, forming a system of benchmarks spanning an entire region. These benchmarks, and therefore the map, must be defined in relation to a fixed reference, called a datum. Unfortunately, there are a number of datums on which maps are based. In order for the coordinates provided by a GPS receiver to be accurate on a map, the GPS must be set to the same datum as the map. Failure to use the correct datum can result in errors of several miles or more.

Most USGS topographic maps use either the North American Datum 1927 (NAD27) or World Geodetic System 1984 (WGS84) datums; the datum is printed on the map margin. GPS uses the WGS84 datum as its worldwide standard. (NAD83 is essentially the same as WGS84.) When you set the GPS receiver to a datum other than WGS84, it corrects the displayed coordinates appropriately. Newer topographic maps should use the WGS84 datum. If a map has a coordinate system but doesn't show the datum, it's reasonably safe to use WGS84.

With your GPS receiver set to the datum and coordinate system used by your map, you are ready to navigate. As an example, let's say you want to drive to the mouth of an interesting canyon. Looking over your maps at home, you can see that the approach drive leaves the highway onto a maintained dirt road. The next turnoff takes you into a maze of unmaintained roads, with numerous junctions, probably all unmarked. If you can find it, you'll eventually end up on an old mining road that leads to the mouth of the canyon. Just to make things more interesting, you know that you won't be able to reach the turnoff from the highway before dark.

You could plot the coordinates of each road junction, and then key them into your GPS receiver. But there's a better way. Using topographic maps and software (see Resources for sources) on your computer, you can quickly and easily create waypoints (position fixes) at each of the road junctions. You also make a list on paper of the waypoint names and the direction you should turn at each. Next, you create a route on the computer containing all the waypoints in order. Finally, you download the route into your GPS receiver.

As you approach the turnoff on the highway, the GPS receiver shows you exactly how far the turnoff is, giving you plenty of time to slow down and find it. (Although you're doing all the work in my example, it is much better and safer to have a passenger handle the navigation chores.) Now, as you proceed along the dirt road, the GPS receiver shows you the next junction. Since the receiver also shows the direction you're going (only while you're moving, though), you can cross-check with the map to make certain you're going in approximately the right direction. Even if there are new roads not shown on your map, the route and waypoints in the GPS help you find the correct junctions and save a lot of time checking out dead ends. If all goes well, you'll find yourself in the mouth of the canyon, even though you can't see it, ready to explore it after camping for the night.

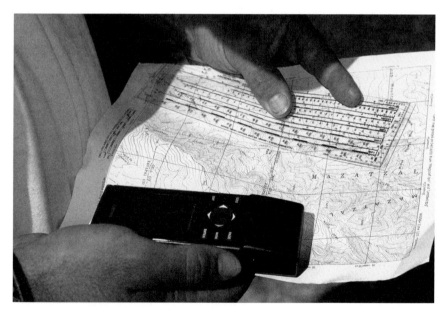

Using a GPS receiver and UTM coordinate scale with a topographic map for navigation

Using GPS When Hiking

Satellite navigation can save a great deal of time and guesswork navigating the desert. It can help you find that elusive turnoff from the highway or an isolated spring. And in some cases, GPS may be the only means of finding your way.

Not too long after I got my first GPS receiver, I planned a hike from a road across a rolling plateau and eventually to the rim of a deep canyon. I planned to walk the rim for several miles, and then walk back across the plateau to my car. I saved the car's position as a waypoint and entered the rim of the canyon as a second waypoint. Sure enough, I struck the rim very close to my intended point. It wasn't until the last leg of the hike that I realized something was seriously wrong with the GPS unit. I knew my car lay approximately 3 miles to the north, but the GPS unit said it was several miles southeast of me, across the canyon. When I plotted the car's saved coordinates on my map, sure enough, it showed my car on the far side of the canyon! I navigated back to the car without difficulty, using the map and local landmarks. But I learned a valuable lesson. Later, an expert friend advised that the GPS receiver may have only had a 2D lock when I saved the car's position. Another possibility is that I accidentally got into edit mode and changed the saved position. Now I always check critical waypoints on the map to see that they make sense.

Determining Your Position

Turn on the GPS receiver and make sure it has a clear view of the sky. Because the satellite signals are extremely weak and line-of-sight, hold the unit as recommended by the manufacturer to get the best reception and remain stationary. After a few seconds, the receiver will lock on to the satellites and display your position. You have a reliable lock and an accurate position when the receiver is locked onto at least four satellites. Most receivers call this a 3D lock, because the receiver then shows your altitude as well. Check the estimated position error reading, or the equivalent, which shows the accuracy of the position computation. It should be at 30 feet or less if you have a good lock. The time required to get a 3D lock varies, depending on how long the receiver has been off and how many satellites the unit can see.

Now, read the coordinates from the receiver and plot them on your map. As I mentioned earlier, UTM is the easiest coordinate system to plot, but you can use latitude and longitude, or any coordinate system used by both your map and GPS unit. Optionally, you can save your position as a named waypoint in the GPS receiver's memory. Make sure you note the name of the waypoint and its purpose, preferably on your map.

If you plan to depend on GPS navigation on a desert trek, make certain you determine the position of your vehicle before leaving it. Save it as a waypoint, and also write down the coordinates just in case.

Finding the Bearing to Your Destination

This works much the same as using a map and compass to determine a bearing. First, read the coordinates of your destination from the map. Then enter the coordinates into your GPS unit as a waypoint. Now, use the GOTO function on the receiver to activate navigation to your destination waypoint. As soon as the receiver has a satellite lock, it will indicate the bearing to the destination. Make certain you have the receiver set to display true north, then use your compass to follow the bearing as described earlier in the "Using Your Compass" section. Don't try to walk a bearing line using the GPS receiver. Doing so runs down your batteries unnecessarily and usually leads to chasing the bearing, or zigzagging, as the bearing readout changes because of the accuracy limitations of the GPS receiver. Instead, stop occasionally, turn on the receiver, and check your position and progress.

Navigation for Biking

The same navigation techniques used for driving back roads and hiking on trails apply to mountain biking. You'll want to use even more care than when driving, because taking a wrong turn costs you energy as well as time. A bike cyclometer is very useful for finding road and trail junctions, and the speedometer function lets you check your rate of progress against the distance to go.

Chapter 6

Gear for the Desert

For hiking in the desert, you need a day pack and good hiking shoes, as well as protective, functional clothing. Backpackers need a larger pack, as well as a sleeping bag, shelter, and cooking equipment. Mountain bikers need appropriate footwear and a pack to carry food, water, and clothing. Vehicle campers don't have to consider weight and bulk but still benefit from the right gear.

You should select gear appropriate for the conditions. On a two-and-a-half-week desert hike through very rugged terrain, my lightweight hiking boots nearly disintegrated. Although I had used these shoes on many hikes, this was the longest trip I'd done with them on especially rocky, abrasive terrain. By the end of the trip, the uppers were more holes than fabric, though they did hang together.

In the wilderness, your comfort and, especially, safety depend on top-quality gear. In a raging thunderstorm, with pounding rain and shrieking wind, a cheap tent is a very poor bargain. During snowfall in a cold fall storm at higher elevations, you won't regret the extra dollars spent on a good sleeping bag.

Take care of your gear—it's your home in the wilderness. A broken pack miles from civilization severely limits your mobility; a ripped tent fly or tarp can mean a miserable, wet experience—or worse. Keep equipment out of the intense desert sun as much as possible. One summer working on a U.S. Forest Service fire lookout, I stored my nylon pack where the summer sun beat on it for 10 or 12 hours a

Water pockets after a storm, Grand Canyon, Great Basin Desert

day, week after week. At the end of the summer, the tough nylon was faded and brittle; when I rubbed it against a boulder, it tore easily and had to be replaced.

The Ten Essentials

The Mountaineers' list of Ten Essentials—the basic items that everyone should have on every backcountry trip—has been updated to reflect a systems approach.

1. Hydration

I discuss water at length in Chapter 3 and elsewhere in the book, but I'll say it again: if there's just one item in your pack on a desert trek, it should be adequate water—carry extra when in doubt.

2. Navigation

Trail signs are sometimes missing or erroneous. Except on easy, familiar treks, always carry a topographic map of the area and be able to read it. Likewise, always carry a good compass and know how to use it. Because the desert is so open and landmarks are visible, you'll rarely need it, but when you do, you'll need it badly, so get a good-quality one that will withstand years of jostling in your pack.

Binoculars are essential for some cross-country work, to look for routes through cliff bands and other obstacles. GPS receivers are rarely essential but can be time-saving and, in some cases, a great help.

See Chapter 5 for navigation details.

3. Sun Protection

The desert sun can produce glare comparable to that of high-altitude snowfields, especially in areas of light-colored stone or sand. Protection from ultraviolet (UV) light is essential, because this wavelength burns skin and causes retina damage. In the desert, except possibly during the winter, the sun will burn even well-tanned skin in a short time. Consider the long-term effects of sun on human skin, especially premature aging and skin cancer. The American Southwest has the highest incidence of skin cancer in the country.

A broad-brimmed sunhat (see the Clothing section, below) and sunscreen are essential. Sunscreens are rated by their sun protection factor (SPF); the higher the number, the more protection you get. During spring, summer, and fall in the desert, use a sunscreen of at least SPF 15. Use sunscreen liberally; don't neglect nose, ears, neck, and bald spots.

A friend and I were near a popular trail in some desert mountains at the end of the day; well after dark, with the temperature already near freezing, we were startled to see a teenage girl trotting along the trail in the glow of her headlamp. She asked us how far it was to the XYZ trailhead. She had set out from her parent's base camp at the ABC trailhead to run a series of trails that led eventually to the XYZ trailhead, where she would run the connecting road back to camp. Though she'd looked at a map in camp, she had neither a map nor a compass with her and had no idea where she was. We determined that she had made a wrong turn at the last trail junction and was now 3 or 4 miles up the wrong trail. We described the trail junction and which way to turn, and she turned around and set off. She apparently made it without trouble, but if she had continued the way she was going, she would have had a 10-mile trip to the wrong trailhead, with no help within at least 5 miles. She would have been in serious trouble, wearing only light running clothing.

Lips are especially susceptible to chapping and burning in the dry desert air; use a good lip balm of SPF 15 or higher. In a pinch, you can use sunscreen on your lips, but keep it away from your eyes.

Sunglasses are a must. The lenses should offer full coverage but still provide ventilation. All glass lenses filter damaging ultraviolet light (UV) to some extent, but plastic lenses must be specially treated or coated; check the label. Cheap sunglasses without UV filtration can actually be worse than no sunglasses at all, because they cause your pupils to open and let in more UV. Because you'll wear your sunglasses for hours at a time, get a good pair that lack optical distortion, which can cause discomfort and headaches.

4. Fire

Carry some means of starting a fire—fire starter and matches or a lighter. A disposable lighter will light when wet and creates a sustained flame. Carry windproof or ordinary wooden kitchen matches carried in a waterproof metal, not plastic, container. Plastic containers melt if the matches catch fire. Windproof matches have an extra large head so they burn longer, which helps in wind. Beware of strike-anywhere matches—they could ignite in your pack from the constant motion of walking.

5. Illumination

Carry a headlamp or flashlight, even if you don't plan to be out after dark. It's easy to miscalculate the time that a hike or ride will take, and even a minor problem can extend your trek into the dark. A reliable flashlight throws enough light to follow a trail at night. A headlamp is the most versatile because it frees your hands and can be used while you're riding a bike. Bring extra batteries and a spare bulb. Solid-state light emitting diode (LED) headlamps and flashlights are extremely reliable, and their diffused white glow is perfect for camp chores and reading; batteries last for 50 hours or more. A dual LED/halogen light can be switched to the halogen bulb when you need a strong beam, at the expense of battery life.

6. First-Aid Kit

Each party should carry a first-aid kit suited to group size and the trip. A pocket-sized first-aid kit containing a few basics is enough for a day hike. A group of six people on a 10-day cross-country trip through a remote area needs a larger kit or several small kits distributed throughout the party. Commercial kits are a good starting point, including items such as adhesive bandages, sterile gauze pads, medical tape, and antibiotic ointment. A dental kit can keep the loss of a filling from ruining a trip. Someone in the group should have a current Red Cross Basic First Aid card or the equivalent.

> *One dark but not stormy night on a solo backpack trip in a desert mountain range, after finishing my dinner I heard muttering from behind me. I watched in amazement as the mutterer, carrying an impossibly dim flashlight, wandered aimlessly across the rocky plateau on which I'd camped. As he wandered closer, I realized he was looking for the main trail, which led to a major trailhead about 4 miles down a nearby canyon. I pointed him in the right direction, and the last I saw of his dim light, he had just about reached the well-traveled main trail, which would be visible in starlight.*

7. Repair Kit

A pocketknife has hundreds of uses—a very good one is for preparing fire-starting tinder in an emergency. Knives with scissors and other tools are standard for hiking, but the type of knife you like is a matter of personal preference. Base your selection on your actual needs in the desert backcountry, and keep the weight as low as you can while still having at least one sturdy, sharp steel blade.

The repair kit should have such items as needles and thread, a general purpose glue, duct tape, ripstop repair tape, and things you need to repair your particular gear. If critical items of your gear, such as your tent or pack, have special parts, such as clevis pins, carry several spares. See the equipment checklist later in this chapter for a sample kit.

8. Nutrition

On treks of a few hours, you might not want to bring lunch, but have a few energy bars or the like in your pack. On longer hikes or rides, always bring some food. Backpackers should have one or two extra meals, in case of delays from injury or weather.

9. Insulation

Carry extra clothing for the worst conditions likely on your adventure. Even if you're out for just a few hours in tee-shirt weather, bring a windbreaker. See the Clothing section later in this chapter for specifics.

10. Emergency Shelter

Carry emergency shelter for the worst conditions you'll likely encounter. A Mylar emergency ("space") blanket weights just 3 ounces and provides protection from wind and rain. See the Shelter section later in this chapter regarding tents.

Footwear

I disagree with the conventional wisdom that the heavier the load, the heavier your boot should be. Weight on your feet costs you more energy, by a large factor, than weight in your pack. In the desert, hiking footwear should be sturdy and protective enough for the terrain.

Likewise, the argument that hiking boots should have ankle support doesn't make sense. Any boot that supports your ankle restricts its movement, which leads to chafing. Instead, to prevent sprains, build up your ankle strength. If you're new to hiking or have not hiked for a while, start out doing day hikes on good trails, and gradually work up to longer hikes, rougher terrain, and heavier loads.

The exact footwear you need depends on experience and personal preference. Some people do long cross-country backpack trips on some of the most rugged desert terrain in the world wearing low-cut running shoes. I prefer a mid-cut light-weight hiker style to keep rocks out of my shoes, but on day hikes or all-trail backpack trips I wear low-cut running or walking shoes. Other hikers prefer a light all-leather hiking boot.

For most desert hiking, you don't have to worry about waterproofness. Breathability is more important, so your feet don't overheat. With proper socks (see below), your feet can get wet and still stay warm. If you encounter snow and freezing temperatures, a lightweight hiking boot made with a waterproof/breath-able fabric such as Gore-Tex makes the most sense.

On some desert canyon hikes you may be wading a fair amount, so you'll need amphibious footwear. One approach is running or walking shoes that have a mesh upper for quick drainage. Another is the now classic river-running sandals such as Tevas. These strap securely to your feet and have high-traction soles designed for wet surfaces, ideal for canyon wading. Carry a pair of lightweight running or camp shoes for chilly evenings in camp.

Opposite: Slot canyon, Grand Canyon, Great Basin Desert

Socks

Cotton socks might be okay for short, casual desert walks in benign weather, but for serious hiking you need good wool or synthetic socks of at least medium thickness. Cotton loses most of its insulating, padding bulk when wet and is very slow to dry. Moist skin contributes to blisters, plus wet socks are dangerous during wet, cold weather. Wool and synthetics such as polypropylene and polyester wick moisture away from your skin and retain their insulating properties when wet. In warm weather, medium or thick socks help insulate your foot from the hot ground. Wool is more resilient than synthetic socks, although wool with nylon and Spandex extends the life of the sock and improves the fit.

Many hikers prefer to wear a thin liner sock under a heavier outer sock; the two layers help prevent blisters by rubbing against each other, rather than your skin. If the inner sock is made of a fabric such as polypropylene, it can wick moisture away from your skin and into the outer sock, where it gradually evaporates.

You might think that you'd want to wear only thin socks in hot weather, but I like the padding of medium to heavy socks. If it's really hot, you can forgo socks altogether and wear river sandals, at the cost of some foot protection.

Clothing

In the backcountry, you need to be comfortable in a wide range of weather conditions, from hot and dry to windy, wet, and cold. Buying good-quality clothing is important. I once set out on a 14-day desert backpack trip wearing a pair of pants I bought at a thrift store. The fabric was so worn that it tore on every bush and rock. By the end of the trip, I was wearing mostly holes held together with a bit of fabric.

I prefer muted colors in the backcountry so that I have minimum visual impact on other desert trekkers. Wear a bright layer when you do want to be seen, such as during hunting season. Dark-colored clothing dries more quickly, but light-colored clothing reflects some of the sun's heat.

Fibers

Synthetic fibers outperform natural fibers in nearly every case. Wool still holds its own for socks, though synthetics such as acrylic are making inroads (see the preceding section). Cotton is very slow to dry and loses much of its insulating value when wet. A soaking-wet cotton tee shirt does feel good on a hot desert day—until the evening chill sets in.

Down, the fluffy underfeathers of waterfowl, is such an efficient insulator that it still has a place in the backcountry. High-quality down lofts to 800 cubic inches or more per ounce, and no synthetic insulator comes close, despite decades of research by fiber manufacturers. Although not as water-resistant as polyester fleece and pile, down does repel water. But once down *is* wet, it takes a long time to dry, so in the desert it is best for insulating sleeping bags and garments that won't be worn on the trail.

Synthetic fibers such as polypropylene (polypro) or treated polyester (poly), which are sold under various trade names such as Capilene, are very good at wicking moisture away from your skin. Synthetic pile and fleece fabrics, which are made from polyester under several trade names such as Polartec, are efficient insulators and absorb very little water. Nylon fabrics are strong and light, unexcelled for outer shell garments. Various treatments make nylon shells water-repellent or waterproof while retaining at least some breathability.

A *windproof fabric* is either tightly woven or coated so that wind doesn't pass through. For instance, mosquito netting has large openings between the threads so that air passes through easily; nylon taffeta is densely woven so that very little air passes through. A *waterproof fabric* is impermeable to liquid water. Polyurethane-coated nylon is completely waterproof; nylon treated with a water-repellent finish is far less waterproof. Although the water-repellent finish causes water droplets to bead up and run off, water under even slight pressure is forced through the fabric. A *breathable fabric* lets moisture in the form of water vapor, a gas, pass through. Polyurethane-coated nylon is not breathable; a cotton tee shirt is very breathable.

On the last day of a strenuous late fall Grand Canyon backpack trip, my friend and I climbed 4,000 feet to the rim on a steep trail. He wore a cotton tee shirt and socks; I wore polypro sock liners and a lightweight polypro underwear top. When we stopped for a break, my companion immediately started to chill off and reached for his down jacket; I didn't need my jacket unless the break was prolonged. We arrived at the 7,000-foot rim at sunset, and the temperature was already below freezing. The only places where my polypro top was moist were where the pack pressed on it, and these areas dried in a few minutes. My friend's cotton tee shirt was soaked with sweat, and he couldn't wait to get out of it. For the drive out, normally I change to dry socks so my feet don't get chilled, but my feet felt so warm and dry in the polypro liners that I left them on—and my feet stayed warm. That experience convinced me of the value of wicking and fast-drying synthetics.

Great progress has been made in creating a fabric combining these traits to various degrees. Gore-Tex, the best-known waterproof/breathable/windproof fabric, is a Teflon membrane with pores small enough to block liquid water droplets, yet large enough to allow remarkable breathability. Because the membrane is not durable, it is laminated to an outer layer of nylon fabric for protection and support. An inner lining is either laminated to the membrane or sewn in. The outer fabric ranges from heavy-duty nylon duck to extremely light nylon taffeta or ripstop. Although Gore-Tex was the original, there are now several competing waterproof/breathable fabrics.

Layering

To minimize weight and bulk while still having enough clothing for weather extremes, dress in layers. Several layers of clothing are warmer and more versatile than one heavy one because the layers trap additional insulating air between them, and the various layers can be combined differently to suit conditions. Wear the layers in whatever combinations keep you comfortable.

In the morning around a chilly camp, you might wear lightweight poly underwear, a shirt, pants, a down or fleece jacket, and a fleece hat and gloves. If you break camp in the rain, wear your shell parka and pants. Setting off on the day's walk, you might wear all your layers at first, but unless it's very cold, you'll soon be down to a poly top plus a shirt and pants. You can regulate your comfort with gloves and a fleece hat. As the day warms up, trade the fleece hat for a sun hat and strip down to regular underwear plus a shirt and pants. Although shorts and bare shoulders are comfortable in hot weather, use extreme caution when you expose bare skin to the desert sun for any length of time.

From the skin out, the basic four layers are inner, outer, insulating, and outer shell.

Inner layer. Lightweight underwear provides extra insulation for cold conditions, and it wicks moisture into the outer layers of your clothes, where it evaporates. Polypro and treated polyester are best, because they wick efficiently and dry quickly. Treated polyester retains its shape better than polypro and doesn't absorb body odors as readily. When you don't expect serious cold weather, a poly short-sleeve tee shirt and underwear briefs do the job; for women, poly briefs and sport bras wick moisture better than cotton or nylon underwear. On colder trips, take a long-sleeve top and long underwear bottoms, which are especially handy at cold camps; you can change into a fresh, dry layer for wearing in your sleeping bag.

Poly liner gloves are useful in very cold weather. They not only wick when worn under heavier gloves but, worn alone, also help keep your fingers warm for delicate tasks.

Outer layer. Shirt and pants are your normal outer layer during the day when you're active. Both should be lightweight, quick-drying, and tough enough to withstand tearing from brush and abrasion from rocks and the ground. Long-sleeved shirts are better in brush; you can always roll up the sleeves. Polyester or brushed nylon are best. Some people use medium- or expedition-weight poly underwear for this layer, which works on trails but not so well when moving cross-country, where the soft weave snags easily on brush.

Many desert rats like to hike in shorts when brush and weather permit; an efficient solution is pants whose legs zip off to convert into shorts. Another solution is extremely light poly shorts made for river runners and water sports.

Insulating layer. A medium-weight jacket is normally worn only at rest stops or around camp. Choose polyester fleece or pile if you expect significant wet weather. For normal desert weather, a down jacket with a light nylon shell is practical. For warm weather, when nighttime temperatures will be mild, a fleece or down vest may do the trick with even less weight and bulk. Insulating pants are rarely needed on desert trips.

Medium-weight fleece gloves are a good compromise between warmth and dexterity. Mittens are warmer, but are needed only on the coldest trips, perhaps a hike into the higher desert mountains in late fall.

Up to half your body's heat is lost through your head. A fleece watch cap or balaclava that covers your ears is versatile. A hooded down or fleece jacket can protect your head, but the hood doesn't turn with your head and usually can't be worn by itself. In warm weather, the sun beating on your unprotected head is uncomfortable and dangerous. A broad-brimmed sun hat is one answer, but the wide brim can interfere with your pack. Another approach is the desert rat hat—a baseball-style cap with a sun curtain hanging from the sides and rear to protect your ears and neck.

Outer shell layer. This layer protects you from wind and rain. Ideal shell garments are made from a waterproof/breathable fabric, which protects you from wind and rain while allowing body moisture to escape. Even though no waterproof/breathable fabric is perfectly waterproof, windproof, or breathable, what moisture does get in or is trapped inside is handled so well by the current generation of high-tech synthetic inner clothes that the resulting combination is nothing short of a revolution in comfort and safety in adverse conditions.

A waterproof/breathable shell parka should have an attached hood for maximum protection and be designed with minimum seams and openings. Because stitches are a leakage point, all seams should be factory-sealed. Openings for zippers and pockets should be guarded from rain and wind with storm flaps. Draw cords at the hood, wrists, and hem or waist can close these openings in cold or windy weather. A matching set of waterproof/breathable pants completes the outer shell layer.

Packs

You'll need a pack to carry your gear for all but the shortest hikes in the desert. Spend time selecting a comfortable pack, and try it with a load. When you get it home, load your new pack with typical gear; water can substitute for food. Adjust the pack carefully according to the manufacturer's instructions. Take a few walks around the block and fine-tune the adjustments. Any discomfort on such an easy walk will be worse in the backcountry, so be sure of your new pack before you use it in the field. Most shops and mail-order suppliers will let you return an unused pack.

The load test also ensures your pack is big enough for your gear. Pack volume is rated in cubic inches or liters, but measuring methods vary, so use the manufacturer's volume as only a general guide. The conventional wisdom is that if you get a larger pack than you need, you'll fill it up with things you don't need; thus, a common mistake is getting a pack that's too small, which forces you to attach gear to the outside. This makes an awkward load that snags on brush and rocks and throws you off balance. You can buy a selection of packs for different-length trips, but if you want just one pack for day hikes and another for multiday trips, buy a little bigger than you think you'll need, then review your gear carefully before each trip to eliminate unnecessary stuff.

Lumbar and Day Packs

Lumbar, or fanny, packs. These ride at the rear of a waist belt and don't have shoulder straps. They are great for short hikes and bike rides when you don't need much water and gear. They're popular for photography and bird-watching, when you want frequent access to gear, guidebooks, or notes. Lumbar packs leave your back free and cool, and some have water-bottle carriers on the sides of the main pack bag, so you can reach your water without moving or opening the pack. If the weather is warm, though, water bottles stored outside the pack absorb sunlight and make the water hot and unpalatable. You can get to the contents of a lumbar pack without taking it off, by loosening the belt slightly and twisting it around to the front.

Day packs. Longer day hikes, especially when weather threatens or you have to carry a lot of water, require a larger pack with shoulder straps. Look for a day pack with a waist belt, which stabilizes the pack on tricky ground. Day packs are either top-loading or back-loading. Top loaders have a draw-cord top and a flap that buckles over the top to keep rain out. They can be overloaded because you can scrunch the gear down as you pull the draw cord tight. Back loaders are designed to be laid flat, and they open with a zipper around the sides and top. They let you get at your gear without digging down through the pack's contents to find something, but they can't be loaded too full without straining the zipper. Both styles usually have outside pockets to stash small items where you can easily find them.

Alpine packs. Designed for mountaineers, these are streamlined with few outside pockets. Some desert hikers prefer them because they are less likely to snag on brush and rocks. Detachable accessory pockets are sometimes available.

If you use a hydration system, get a pack with a built-in hydration pocket and hose port. The pocket keeps your water reservoir in place against your back, helping to keep the pack's center of gravity closer to your own, which makes it easier to balance on tricky terrain.

Hydration Packs

These packs are designed around hydration systems and have a built-in water reservoir. Water buried in your pack stays cool, and you tend to drink more often because access is so easy. However, most hydration packs have limited capacity for other gear, and some have reservoirs too small for long day hikes in warm weather. A solution is to carry more water in regular bottles and refill the reservoir as needed.

Multiday Packs

Overnight packs have larger capacity to accommodate camping gear, and most use a frame to support the load and transmit much of the weight to your hips. They should have a sophisticated shoulder harness to keep the pack close to your body, and a well-designed hip belt to carry heavier loads. Lift straps on the tops of the shoulder straps and stabilizer straps at the sides of the hip belt fine-tune the pack's fit for different conditions. Consult the manufacturer's instructions to set it up correctly, and know how to adjust it for changing loads and conditions. A good outdoor shop can help.

Most multiday packs fit different torso lengths, and some are designed specifically for women. If the pack is too tall or too short, it won't distribute the load properly. When I worked in outdoor shops, many customers who complained of uncomfortable packs were using packs that were too large for them, loaned or handed down from a friend or family member.

There are two types of multiday packs: external frame or internal frame.

External frames. The pack bag and harness are attached to a frame made from aluminum tubing (or sometimes magnesium or plastic). The pack rides on mesh bands stretched across the frame, which allows air to circulate across your back. The pack bag, held in shape by the frame and usually loaded with pockets and compartments, is easy to load and organize, but it does tend to feel top heavy. It's tempting to overload an external frame pack by lashing gear to the frame, but such overloads are awkward and snag on brush easily.

Internal frames. One or more vertical stays, made from aluminum or carbon fiber, insert into pockets inside the pack. Internal-frame packs hug your back like a limpet and ride lower, so they don't affect your balance as much as an external frame pack. Most have a lower, slimmer profile, and they don't catch on low branches or brush as much. Internals are also easier to haul or lower when you're faced with a bit of rock scrambling.

Construction and Materials

Most packs are made of nylon fabrics of various weights and styles. Nylon is premier because it is very strong for its weight. Nylon duck is traditional, but it lacks abrasion resistance. Cordura and other nylon fabrics with better abrasion resistance have been developed. Although these are too heavy to use for an entire pack, they are used as reinforcement in critical wear areas.

The pack should be well sewn, with extra stitches or bar tacking at stress areas such as shoulder-strap and hip-belt attachments.

Pack Covers

Although most packs are built from waterproof materials, heavy or prolonged rain will get through seams and openings. A separate rain cover made from light-weight, waterproof nylon helps gear stay dry. In a pinch, you can use a large plastic trash bag, though brush will shred it quickly.

Loading a Pack

Load all packs with the heaviest items close to your back. This keeps the pack's center of gravity close to yours, which means you can walk with a more comfortable upright posture. Usually water, food, and stove fuel are the heaviest items.

Pack external frames with the heaviest items in the upper half. Many external frames have a three-quarter-length pack bag, leaving the bottom of the frame free for attaching your sleeping bag. This automatically moves the center of gravity upward. Don't pack the weight too high, or the pack will become top heavy.

Pack internal frames and day packs with the weight fairly low, which makes you more stable on rough terrain.

If your pack is only partially full, use the compression straps to pull the load in toward your back. Or stuff your down or fleece jacket in loose after everything else is loaded; it not only fills the excess space but also insulates your water and food from the desert heat. If you carefully put the pack in the shade at each rest stop, its contents will stay remarkably cool.

Pack pockets are great for organizing small items, such as snacks, headlamps, maps, and other things you want readily to hand. Some packs have pockets that you can reach with the pack on.

Sleeping Bags and Pads

Don't skimp on your sleeping bag. Uncomfortable, cold nights will ruin your trip.

Shape. The classic mummy bag is the most efficient design in terms of warmth for the weight carried, because there is no excess material. Rectangular and semirectangular bags have a little more room; rectangular bags are fine for car camping, when weight isn't a concern. A good bag has a hood you can draw around your head to close off drafts. Some bags have a draft collar just below shoulder level, which keeps drafts out without having to close the hood.

Fill. Sleeping bags are filled with either down or a variety of synthetic, polyes-ter-based insulations. Down is the warmest insulator for its weight, despite decades of search for a synthetic replacement. Down is more costly, and although it is difficult to get it wet, it is hard to dry in the field. Down is also far more durable than any of the synthetics—if cared for, down usually outlasts the sleeping bag's shell. Synthetic fills are initially less expensive; they retain most of their warmth when wet; and they are hypoallergenic.

Season. For most desert backpacking and camping, you need a three-season bag. If you tend to camp primarily during the warmer months, you can get by with a summer bag. A winter bag is overkill in the desert, because desert winters (except on the highest peaks) are as warm as spring or fall in less-arid regions.

Temperature rating. Use these to compare bags by the same manufacturer only, because there's no consistency across the industry. Keep in mind whether you sleep warm or cold—individuals vary, and just because a bag is rated to, say, 10 degrees F doesn't mean it will keep everyone warm to that temperature.

Loft. A better way of comparing the warmth of sleeping bags is by measuring their loft, or thickness, when laid flat. All sleeping bag insulators work by trapping tiny pockets of air between the fibers, and the thicker the insulation, the warmer the bag. Three-season bags should have a loft of 6 or 7 inches; a summer-weight bag should have 4 to 5 inches of loft.

Care. Take care of your bag on each trip. Avoid eating or drinking around it, and keep it away from water and dew. Don't bury your head inside the bag on cold nights; moisture from your breath will condense on the insulation, making you even colder. Instead, wear a watch cap or balaclava to reduce the significant amount of heat lost by your head. If necessary, wear lightweight long underwear inside the bag for extra warmth.

Storage. At home, always store a sleeping bag loose, either hung up in a closet or other dry place or in an oversize, breathable storage sack. Never store a bag in its stuff sack. Insulations lose their loft if left tightly stuffed, and down will mildew.

Sleeping Pads

A sleeping pad provides insulation from the cold ground plus varying degrees of comfort. A three-quarter-length pad, around 48 inches long, minimizes weight and bulk while providing padding and insulation for your hips and shoulders. Use extra clothing to pad and insulate your feet and legs. A full-length pad is luxurious when car camping.

Closed-cell foam pads. Lightest and simplest, these are relatively thin—usually 0.25 to 0.5 inch thick—and have tiny gas bubbles trapped in the foam. Retaining most of their thickness under body weight, they are very effective insulators, waterproof, and, even more useful in the desert, puncture-proof. Because the foam doesn't compress, closed-cell pads are bulky when rolled up. Simple designs are simply cut sheets of flat foam in various thicknesses and lengths. More sophisticated pads are molded in an egg-crate pattern, which increases the thickness without adding weight.

Open-cell foam pads. When these pads are unrolled, the cells inflate with air. Open-cell pads compress under body weight, so they have to be thicker to provide enough padding and insulation—usually about 1.5 inches. Because the open cells suck up water as well as they do air, the pad needs a waterproof cover. Open-cell pads are more comfortable but also bulkier and heavier to carry.

Air mattresses. If properly inflated, these are very comfortable, but, except for specialized situations (such as canyon hiking where they are useful for floating your pack across pools), air mattresses have fallen out of favor in the desert. They attract cactus spines like a magnet; I've never completed a desert backpack trip without having to repair a puncture. An air mattress provides very little insulation because air circulates in the chambers, convecting away your body heat.

Self-inflating foam pads. These are essentially air mattresses filled with low-density open-cell foam, which provides insulation and stabilizes the pad's thickness, so they need be only about 1 to 1.5 inches thick to provide great comfort and insulation. Because the foam is low density, it compresses readily for packing when the valve is opened. These pads fill themselves with air when unrolled with the valve open. You might have to top the pad off with a few puffs of air, but it's nothing like the sustained effort needed to inflate an air mattress. More sophisticated self-inflating pads use cored foam to save weight and bulk. Self-inflating foam pads are less susceptible to cactus punctures than air mattresses.

Leaks. Campfire sparks are especially deadly to air mattresses and self-inflating pads, but at least the large holes made by embers are easy to find. Pinholes from cactus spines let you down slowly and can be maddeningly difficult to find. Check inflatable pads for leaks before leaving home. Check an air mattress by blowing it up firmly, preferably with a pump, then check to see if the mattress goes limp after a few hours. If you've blown it up by mouth, the mattress will lose some pressure as the warm air from your breath cools. When this happens, top it off and watch to see if it goes limp again. Check a self-inflating pad by rolling it up tightly and closing the valve. If the pad unrolls after a couple of hours, it has a leak, possibly more than one. To find tiny holes in either an air mattress or self-inflating pad, blow it up as firm as you can and then submerge one section at a time in a pool of water, such as a bathtub. This can be very difficult to do in the desert backcountry.

Once you locate the leak, which is betrayed by tiny streams of air bubbles, mark it with a pencil, and then remove the pad and allow it to dry thoroughly. Then repair the hole using the manufacturer's repair kit; carry this in the field, too.

Storage. Always store sleeping pads unrolled and uncompressed. A pad compressed for long periods of time tends to lose its resilience. Store self-inflating pads and air mattresses with the valves open to prevent internal mildew.

Shelter

A desert backpacking shelter needs to protect you from rain, wind, insects, sun, and, rarely, snow. Don't skimp on quality—your roof is a poor place to save money.

Opposite: Kelso Dunes, Mojave Desert National Preserve

Tarps

Usually made of nylon taffeta or ripstop with grommets or ties along the edges, a tarp for one to four persons is simple and light, weighing as little as a pound. Used with a plastic or nylon groundsheet, it still weighs less than 3 pounds. A tarp can be used as a sunshade when pitched high to allow plenty of air circulation. A tarp and groundsheet often let you sleep out under the brilliant stars—a glorious experience. But tarps offer no protection from mosquitoes, crawling insects, or reptiles. Avoid using a tarp and groundsheet if you camp in warm weather when insects and snakes are active at night.

A tarp can be set up in different configurations to match the terrain and the weather, from a low, battened-down A-shape to a high, airy canopy. Pitching a tarp requires some thought, especially if the site is unusual or you need protection from a cold wind. Pick the best possible site with natural protection from the wind if a storm is brewing. Openings in dense brush or the lee side of rock outcrops are good.

Bivy Sacks

A bivy sack is essentially a sleeping bag cover with a waterproof bottom and a breathable, or waterproof/breathable, top. More sophisticated designs add no-see-um netting and perhaps a pole or two to keep the sack off your face. Even the simplest sleeping bag cover adds 10 to 20 degrees F of warmth to your sleeping bag. By itself, a bivy sack is claustrophobic—spending hours or days in one is an experience not to be repeated. But a bivy sack can work well under a tarp in windy weather, keeping wind-driven rain off your sleeping bag. A tarp/bivy combo is still lighter than most tents, especially for solo hikers. A bivy sack can also transform a marginal rock overhang into a comfortable shelter.

Three-Season Tents

A desert tent should be as light as possible, while still having enough room and enough strength to handle desert rain and wind. A three-season tent can handle a bit of snow; four-season tents are only possibly needed for winter mountaineering on the highest desert peaks—a subject outside the scope of this book.

Double or single wall. Most tents are double-walled: the main tent body has a waterproof floor and a breathable, nonwaterproof canopy, and a separate, waterproof fly pitches snugly over the tent for rain protection. A few tents are single-walled, with a canopy made from waterproof/breathable fabric. Double-wall tents work better in the desert: you can leave the fly off for more ventilation on warm, dry nights, and during the day the double wall provides more sun protection. Make sure your tent has factory seam sealing. You can seal seams yourself, using sealant made for your tent fabric, but factory sealing is stronger and lasts the life of the tent.

Freestanding or not. Dome or modified dome tents stand up by themselves once the poles are inserted. Nonfreestanding designs must be pegged to the ground to stay up, but because they generally have fewer poles, they're usually lighter. Any tent must be staked securely to the ground if there's a chance of strong wind, so the dome's advantages aren't that great.

Vestibules. Some rain flies have vestibules for a dry area outside the canopy. In prolonged bad weather, this makes it easier to get in and out of the tent without getting the interior wet, and it also provides a place for wet and muddy raingear and boots. You can also cook in the vestibule if necessary. Vestibules add weight and bulk, and keep in mind that prolonged storms are not common in the North American deserts. As an alternative, you can use a tarp to make an expansive vestibule—especially luxurious for a car camp or desert base camp.

Poles. Tent poles should be made of lightweight aluminum and be shock-corded together so that pieces can't be lost. Don't whip the poles out to self-assemble; you'll damage the ends of the poles so the segments don't fit together. Avoid tents with fiberglass poles, which are heavy, weak, and a sign of cheap construction. Some such tents don't even have waterproof flies and floors!

Zippers. These should be robust, because if a zipper fails on a door, you won't be able to close the tent. Number 5 coil zippers are the minimum. Double sliders make it possible to open a door or window at either end, and provide versatile ventilation. Hold the zipper together as you close it to avoid stress and wear on the slider. Keep the zipper out of sand and dirt as much as possible; grit wears the slider and eventually prevents the zipper from meshing.

Ventilation. Plenty of ventilation, preferably two doors at opposite ends, is

Hikes by Season

Winter Hikes
Dutchmans-Miners Trail Loop, Superstition Mountains
Lower La Barge Box, Superstition Mountains
Bull Pasture, Organ Pipe Cactus National Monument
Coyote Pass Loop, Tucson Mountains
Pass Mountain Trail, Usury Mountain Park
Kaibab Trail, Grand Canyon
Kelso Dunes, Mojave National Preserve

Fall Hikes
Confluence Overlook, Canyonlands National Park
Mount Charleston Loop, Spring Range

Spring Hikes
Double-O Arch Trail, Arches National Park
Bamhardt–Rock Creek Loop, Mazatzal Mountains
Secret Canyon, Red Rock-Secret Mountain Wilderness

important. All doors, windows, and vents should be covered with no-see-um netting, which is finer meshed than mosquito netting, to keep out tiny gnats. It's not necessary for the nylon canopy itself to close completely; some three-season tents have large netting panels in the walls and roof. Because the tent fly covers the entire canopy, these tents are still rain-proof, and the netting provides more ventilation. If the weather is good, you can leave the fly off for still better ventilation, as well as a view of the sky. Net tents, in which all of the canopy, except for the lower sidewalls, is made from nylon netting, are extremely practical for desert camping.

Cook Gear

In accordance with the Leave No Trace principles, campfires have no place in the desert; besides, it's much easier to cook on a camp stove. However, if you must cook on a fire because of stove failure, running out of fuel, or an emergency, build a small fire only in existing fire rings and only where safe and legally permitted; use small pieces of dead and down wood from outside the camp area. Always put any campfire out by mixing the coals and ashes thoroughly with dirt and repeating until the ashes are cool to the touch. If you can't put your hand in the ashes, the fire is not out. Use water if you are camped near a plentiful source.

Camp Stoves

For desert backpacking, get the lightest, most foolproof design, such as a single-burner bivy stove. You have a choice of fuels (see below). If you're cooking for a large group in a car camp or base camp, use a multi-burner stove or use two or more single-burner stoves. With the latter approach, you have more than one stove in case of failure. Also, when one stove runs out of fuel you don't have to shut down the whole cooking show to refuel, as long as you refuel well away from running stoves and all other open flames.

Gasoline. Gasoline puts out more heat per ounce than butane or propane, and a gallon of white gas costs the same as a 7-ounce canister of compressed gas. Some gasoline stoves can run on unleaded auto gas, and some can even run on kerosene and jet fuel, which is valuable in areas where white gas is difficult to find. If you run your stove on auto gas, use plenty of ventilation to avoid inhaling the fumes, which contains poisonous additives.

Spilled gasoline is dangerous. Gasoline fumes can explode, especially in a confined space. Gasoline stoves require priming, which discourages turning the stove off and on. Priming covers the burner with soot, which gets on hands, face, and gear unless you carry the stove in a stuff sack or protective box. Gasoline leaking from a fuel bottle soaks through plastic bags and waterproof nylon, and it can contaminate food beyond use.

Propane. Because of its higher pressure, propane must be stored in heavy tanks so it is most practical for vehicle camps. In large quantities, propane is cheaper than butane. Propane stoves are clean, burn hot, and light instantly.

Compressed gas. Lightweight compressed-gas stoves use butane with a small amount of propane added to increase cold-weather performance. Pure butane vaporizes at about 32 degrees F, and at colder temperatures gas pressure and performance fall off. Butane/propane stoves are clean and easy to operate. Some even have piezoelectric lighters built in.

Transporting. Gasoline stoves with internal fuel tanks, empty fuel containers that have contained fuel, and propane tanks and butane canisters are classed as hazardous materials and cannot be transported by air, either as baggage or freight. Check with the airline before shipping or carrying new, empty containers, and plan to buy fuel at your destination.

Windscreens. Even a slight breeze diverts much of the heat output from a stove burner, so cooking not only takes forever but your fuel consumption goes up as well. Windscreens vary in design from separate foil rings to complete enclosures. Never use a windscreen that completely encloses the burner on a stove with the burner mounted on the fuel tank. This will cause the fuel tank to overheat and possibly explode. Component stoves can safely use a windscreen that totally encloses the burner because the fuel tank is separated from the burner by a flexible fuel line. Such a windscreen is extremely effective.

Conventional windscreens won't help much if the wind is strong, so pick a sheltered stove site, such as the lee of several large boulders. You can also build a stove shelter by placing large, flat slabs of rock away from the stove, and allow plenty of ventilation. Feel the fuel tank with your hand occasionally to check for overheating. If the tank is more than warm to the touch, turn the stove off immediately.

Vestibule cooking. *Never cook in a tent.* All stoves give off carbon monoxide, a deadly, odorless gas. A tent closed up against a storm with a running stove inside can quickly become a death trap. Lightweight nylon gear, especially sleeping bags, catch fire easily and burn rapidly. If you're stuck in your tent for a long time, cook in the vestibule if you must, and eat munchies and snack foods as much as possible. Cooking and eating in a tent also increase the likelihood that mice and other pests will chew their way in.

Pots and Utensils

Keep pots, pans, and eating gear simple, unless you enjoy washing dishes in camp. For two people, a couple of quart-sized pots are plenty. Larger groups need larger pots, but consider cooking in several subgroups, each with their own stove and cook gear. Keeping cooking groups small greatly simplifies trip planning and logistics. Most camp meals can be eaten with a spoon and a large cup.

Elaborate camp cookery is beyond the scope of this book, but plenty of other books have been written on the subject. See the Recommended Reading appendix.

Other Important Items

Personal items might include spare eyeglasses, if you have prescription lenses or contact lenses, and any medications and personal hygiene articles. A small comb can keep those greasy locks under control, especially if your hair is long. A comb is also useful for removing cactus burrs.

Watch

You can roughly determine the time from the position of the sun, but a watch makes life a lot easier—especially if the sun is hidden by thick clouds. With a watch, you can accurately gauge your progress toward important goals, such as the turnaround point on a day hike, the next spring, or your planned campsite. Get a good solid-state, electronic watch, not a wind-up. I accidentally let a wind-up watch run down on the third day of a rough, 10-day cross-country desert hike, which was annoying because I needed to keep accurate track of my progress toward widely spaced springs.

Toilet Paper

Some plants, such as juniper branches, can be used, but it's much better to just carry some of the real stuff. I usually carry a partial roll of dense, non-fluffy paper such as Scott or a traveler's pack of tissues in a zipper plastic bag. (Dry toilet paper is also useful in starting an *emergency* campfire.) In certain areas you may have to carry out used toilet paper; use a plastic zipper-locking bag and some baking soda.

Insect Repellent

Although mosquitoes, gnats, and other bothersome insects are not common in most desert areas, they can be a problem after prolonged rains or near permanent water. Bring a small bottle of DEET, which is the most effective. Lotion-type repellents with a low concentration of DEET are more pleasant than concentration DEET and seem to be effective for most people.

Don't underestimate the value of knowing the stars. I once navigated across 3 miles of dense pinyon-juniper forest in the Great Basin Desert using a bright star to maintain my course despite continuous deviations around small trees. I hit my target—the road junction where my car was parked—dead on. Now I would probably use GPS, but the sight of that star would still be comforting.

Car Keys

If you drive to the trailhead, carry or stash a spare set of keys. I keep a spare set in my first-aid and repair kits at all times. On long treks with several people in the party, I give my main set of keys to another person to carry. Or find a place on your vehicle to secure a spare set of keys, but choose the site very carefully because car thieves know the secret hiding places. Wire the keys securely in place using aviation safety wire, which is designed to withstand prolonged flexing and vibration. Ask a small-airplane mechanic at your local airport for a short length. Avoid magnetic holders—they fall off on dirt roads.

Wallet

On anything longer than a short, easy stroll, I secure my wallet in a zippered pack pocket. On backpack trips I carry a small stuff sack into which I place paper money, driver's license, emergency contact card, credit card, and debit card.

Amusements

Nonessentials can be entertaining. For instance, I enjoy having a thermometer along to see if the night really was as cold as it felt or if the temperature at high noon is truly scorching.

I always carry a notebook, pencil, and pen for making field notes, on maps as well as in the notebook. When I'm mapping a trail or doing serious photography, I carry a tiny digital voice recorder so I can make notes without stopping.

I usually carry a paperback book (or electronic substitute); I find the temporary escape from the trip very refreshing.

A portable game such as chess or a miniature deck of cards can be very enjoyable when you're stuck in camp by the weather. I once lost 26 chess games in a row sitting under a tarp with a friend waiting for the afternoon heat to abate.

I usually carry a star chart. Desert nights in the dry air bring out the stars in a blaze of glory that you have to see to believe. Before I'd really learned the night sky, I carried a small plastic planisphere. These can be set for the local date and time, showing the sky as it appears at the moment, which makes it a lot easier for a beginner to locate the stars, constellations, and planets. Nowadays, I carry a bandanna with a sky map silk-screened on it, a small whole-sky map photocopied from a night-sky field guide, or a very detailed star chart loaded on my backpacking PDA.

Field guidebooks are available for just about everything, from weather to desert flowers to butterflies to birds, and yes, stars. Usually I make notes and refer to the guides back at home, but if I expect something exceptional I'll carry one along. You can carry a selection of field guides in your car.

Photographic Equipment

If you're exploring the desert by vehicle, bring as much camera gear as you want. Even on a day hike—especially one devoted to photography—you can bring a full-size tripod, a couple of camera bodies, and a selection of lenses. If you're backpacking or mountain biking, of course you'll have to minimize the weight and bulk of your photo gear.

Film cameras. Unfortunately, very few of the compact, self-contained point-and-shoot film cameras allow you any technical control over the shot. If you can't find a point-and-shoot that gives you the control you need, consider one of the lighter electronic single-lens-reflex (SLR) camera bodies. When fitted with a wide-range zoom lens, it is a film camera with both automatic and manual modes, at a weight about twice that of a good point-and-shoot.

Film. Photographers shooting for fine art or publication purposes have traditionally shot fine-grained but slow slide films, such as Fuji Velvia, which require a tripod in many situations. To avoid the weight of a tripod, use faster color-negative film, which has less grain than fast slide film. Newer slide films, such as Fuji Velvia 100F, Provia 400F, and Kodak's new ISO 100 Ektachromes, promise both fine grain and higher speeds than older slide films.

Digital cameras. Advanced digital point-and-shoots usually offer a full range of manual and automatic control, comparable to SLR cameras. You can't change lenses, but many of these cameras have a wide zoom range as well as good macro (close-up) capability. High-end digital SLRs (DSLRs) now capture as much detail as film, while at the other end of the spectrum, basic digital point-and-shoot cameras are amazingly light and compact.

Memory cards. With a digital camera, a few tiny memory cards can capture hundreds or thousands of images, plenty for the longest trek. Using the camera's electronic display, you can see the image as the sensor sees it and review your photos as you shoot them or in the evening at camp.

Batteries. Digital cameras use up batteries, especially if you make much use of the display screen or the flash. Look carefully at a digital camera's batteries before buying it, especially for backpacking. Ideally, it should use both high-capacity throw-away batteries, usually lithium, and rechargeable batteries such as nickel metal hydride (NiMH). If you use rechargeable batteries when you have a way of charging them (home charger, vehicle charger, or solar panel), digital photography is just about free. On a backpack trip, lithium batteries are expensive, but they last five times longer than alkaline batteries and are half the weight. My current advanced digital point-and-shoot usually lasts for a couple of days of serious photography, without much use of the flash, on one set of NiMH batteries. Preliminary tests indicate that two sets of lithiums, which weigh exactly the same as a set of NiMH batteries, should last for a 10-day hike.

Heat and dust. Keep film, especially exposed film, in the original airtight canisters deep in your pack during the heat of the day. Never change film in direct sunlight; use the shade of your body to shield the open camera and film. Keep dust and sand out of cameras and lenses by always keeping them in a camera case or stuff sack when not in use. If you do get sand in your camera, don't attempt to operate it—that will just cause further damage. Label it "sand in camera" and get it to a repair shop. Digital camera sensors are especially sensitive to dust, which shows up as specks in the image. If you have a digital SLR, avoid changing lenses in a dusty environment. Shoot an occasional shot of the sky, and magnify it on the screen to look for dust spots. If the sensor does become dusty, carefully clean it according to the manufacturer's instructions.

Techniques

Because of the strong, often harsh light, desert photography is an entire subject in itself. This section points out just some of the problems—and rewards. See the Recommended Reading list.

Light. Both film and digital camera sensors capture a very limited range of light intensity compared to the human eye. Black-and-white film has the greatest range, about 9 or 10 exposure value (EV) steps, whereas color negative film, transparency film, and digital sensors have less range. The human eye can see in bright desert sunlight at one extreme as well as in starlight, which can be a million times dimmer. So the fundamental problem the desert photographer faces is how to capture on film or sensor what the eye sees. Remember that you are immersed in the scene, experiencing not just the narrow slice of landscape seen in the viewfinder but also the complete sweeping panorama, as well as the sounds, smell, and feel of the desert at that moment. It's a real challenge to capture a photo that conveys this to the viewer.

Golden hours. Begin by working with the light. During the outdoor photographer's classic golden hours—the hour after sunrise and the hour before sunset—the soft desert light takes on a golden tinge, because the sunlight is slanting through a great deal more atmosphere than at midday. Contrast is often reduced to something the camera can handle. During spring and fall, the golden hours extend for a longer period, and in winter, the light is soft most of the day. By shooting landscapes during these periods, you can get photos with texture, depth, and detail.

Clouds. Thinly overcast days are ideal for close-ups of desert flowers, cactus, and other desert details that need even light without strong shadows. Don't neglect bad weather, either. Unusual cloud formations, distant thunderstorms, and other weather effects make the sky much more interesting than the usual deep desert blue.

People. Take plenty of shots of your fellow trekkers. Although landscape and nature shots are wonderful for portraying desert wilderness, photos of people enjoying the backcountry are always popular. Small point-and-shoot cameras are excellent for catching people in the act.

Wildlife. On a long hike, you can't carry the long lenses and heavy tripods that are standard for wildlife work, but don't ignore what drops into your lap. If you have the time to stay in one place, try quietly hanging out near a spring or tank, especially at dawn or dusk. Even during the cooler months, most animals and birds are more active in the morning and evening than they are during the day.

Equipment Checklist

This is a list of possible items to consider for various desert trips, including exploring by car, biking, hiking, and backpacking. You would never take all of this gear on any given trip.

Footwear
- hiking boots
- socks
- staff

Pack
- pack
- rain cover
- accessory pockets
- day pack
- lumbar pack

Sleeping
- sleeping bag with stuff sack
- sleeping pad with repair kit
- ground sheet
- tarp
- bivy sack
- tent

Essentials
- water
- first-aid/repair kit
- knife
- lighter or matches
- headlamp or flashlight with extra batteries and bulb
- sun hat
- sunscreen lotion
- lip balm
- sunglasses
- maps
- compass
- watch
- toilet paper
- insect repellent
- car keys

- personal essentials
- toothbrush with toothpaste
- floss

Kitchen
- stove with fuel
- pots
- frying pan
- cup
- bowl
- spoon
- pot gripper
- can opener
- salt container
- butter container
- lighter
- soap
- iodine tablets
- coffee filters
- trash bag
- pot cleaner
- Handiwipe

Clothing
- pants
- shorts
- belt
- poly shirt or tee shirt
- wicking thermal underwear, lightweight
- wicking underwear
- bandanna
- sun hat
- balaclava
- down jacket
- pile jacket
- shell jacket, waterproof/breathable

- shell pants, waterproof/breathable
- gloves

Accessories
- GPS receiver
- thermometer
- binoculars
- notebook with pencil and pen
- comb
- wallet
- paperback book
- game
- star chart
- field guides

Photography
- camera with spare batteries
- camera case
- walking stick monopod adapter
- mini-tripod
- cable release
- film or memory cards
- lens paper
- brush
- blower
- filters

Mountain Biking
- bicycle
- tool kit
- patch kit
- spare tube
- pump
- water bottles or hydration system
- headlamp

Equipment Checklist (Continued)

❑ tail light
❑ racks
❑ panniers
❑ trunk bag
❑ seat bag
❑ handlebar bag
❑ pack

First-Aid and Repair Kit
❑ medical tape
❑ gauze pads
❑ gauze roll
❑ bandages
❑ felt moleskin

❑ single-edge razor
   blade
❑ elastic bandage
❑ aspirin or analgesic
❑ antacid tablets
❑ antihistamine tablets
❑ dental kit
❑ whistle
❑ mini-lighter
❑ signal mirror
❑ space blanket
❑ survival booklet
❑ screws
❑ nylon thread
❑ needles

❑ safety pins
❑ ripstop tape
❑ Barge's cement
❑ tweezers
❑ duct tape

Supplies in Vehicle
❑ extra maps
❑ extra clothing
❑ extra food
❑ extra water
❑ guidebooks
❑ cord/rope
❑ jumper cables
❑ tools

Chapter 7

Driving the Back Roads and Biking the Trails

riving desert back roads, or even desert highways, is a great way to begin exploring the North American deserts. Especially if you are new to the desert, you can get a feel for desert country without having to commit too much time or buy specialized equipment. Mountain biking is a very enjoyable way to explore desert backroads and trails.

Can I Get There from Here?

Before starting a desert trip by vehicle, consider the roads you'll be driving. Under normal conditions, an ordinary car can be driven safely over the many maintained dirt or gravel desert roads. You can drive an ordinary car on some unmaintained roads too, but many unmaintained roads require a vehicle with higher clearance than a standard car. As I mentioned earlier, one option is a car-based SUV or all-wheel drive car. Although not as rugged as a truck, these vehicles usually have higher clearance than a standard car, and the four-wheel (4WD) or all-wheel drive gives them a big advantage in loose sand. However, if you plan to explore rocky, steep roads, then you'll need to have a 4WD truck or truck-based SUV that is designed and equipped for travel on rough roads. Most SUVs are not designed for rough roads, so be careful when buying one for desert exploration. Another option is to plan a trip around both a vehicle and a mountain bike. Use the vehicle to get to the end of the good dirt road, and then take to the bike to explore the rougher roads.

Preparation

All desert trips require some advance preparation, even a touring trip that will stick to paved roads. Some desert highways are very remote by the standards of the rest of the country. A prime example is the "Loneliest Road in America," US 50 across the Great Basin Desert.

Planning Ahead

Consult maps and guidebooks at home so you'll know what to expect. For trips to desert national parks or preserves, give the rangers a call to check on road conditions and closures, campground status, and any other changes or restrictions. Another good resource is the park's website. Talk to friends who've been to the area to get a personal feel for the place.

Weathering the Storm

Check the weather forecast before leaving home. Television and radio forecasts, although loosely based on government forecasts, are reinterpreted primarily for city activities and are usually too superficial and broad for backcountry travel. I recommend that you learn a little more about weather and consider using official sources for weather information. Although it is a commercial weather source, the Weather Channel is a good starting point to get the big picture of the weather in the desert you plan to visit. Don't put too much faith in the forecast beyond about 3 days, though. Official government weather information is available from the National Weather Service (NWS) through direct phone calls to a local NWS office, either from a live weather person or via recording. The NWS has an excellent website where you can get detailed weather conditions, forecasts, and climate data for anywhere in the country.

You need to be especially concerned about temperatures. Check both the high and the low that your target area has been experiencing for the last several days, and then look at the forecast for the next couple of days. Desert temperatures typically vary by 40 or 50 degrees F each day. If the highs are running in the 70s, you'll have very pleasant daytime temperatures for driving and side hikes or bike rides, but nighttime temperatures will be very chilly, possibly below freezing. Keep this in mind if you plan to camp. On the other hand, balmy nighttime temperatures usually mean that the days will be scorching. Temperatures in the 90s and higher are unpleasant for hiking and cycling, though they are excellent for exploring deep canyons and for paddling. One technique that works well on hot days is to plan to hike or ride in the morning, while temperatures are still moderate, then explore or drive to a new area during the afternoon heat. Air-conditioned vehicles can be a welcome relief during the afternoon heat, but be aware that you may not be able to use the air conditioning on slow, rocky back roads without overheating the engine.

During the rainy seasons, check to see how much rain has fallen recently, as well as the forecast. A long rainy period in the winter can saturate the ground, setting the conditions for flooding. At the very least, normally dry rivers and creeks may be running and low water crossings may be washed out or unusable for weeks at a time. Playas and salt flats become wet and soft, or they may flood completely. Summer thunderstorms tend to occur in bursts of activity that last several days, and may intensify rapidly, causing dry crossings and even entire roadways to wash out.

Check for the possibility of high winds, especially in the spring. If wind is in the forecast, plan to avoid sandy areas such as the southern Mojave Desert in California and the canyon country of the eastern Great Basin Desert in Utah. Areas with large areas of disturbed soil, such as desert valleys with active or abandoned irrigated farmland, are subject to blinding dust storms.

Snowstorms and winter weather are a consideration when planning a trip to the higher deserts, such as the northern Great Basin Desert, and many of the mountain ranges in the other deserts. The highest desert mountains can have snowstorms any time of year, and even the lower ranges get occasional snow.

Desert camp after a winter snowstorm, Grand Canyon, Great Basin Desert

Be Mechanically Sound

Because desert roads are usually remote, your vehicle must be well maintained. Reliability is more important than any other factor when considering a car or truck for desert exploration. Buy a vehicle that has a reliable track record, and have it serviced regularly by a competent mechanic. Because modern vehicles can't be serviced without computerized diagnostics and other specialized tools, most field breakdowns are difficult or impossible to repair. I've owned several vehicles with several hundred thousand miles on them, yet I've confidently taken them on back roads that were up to 100 miles from any town or settlement because I made sure they got preventive maintenance.

Pay special attention to your tires. I've run mud- and snow-rated, steel-belted radial tires for years and rarely get a flat. The important thing is to buy high-quality tires that won't break on the first sharp rock you run over. You also want to have a good spare, preferably not one of the temporary duty tires that many new cars are saddled with. In really remote and rugged areas, consider carrying two spares.

Tools and Repairs

Despite the complexity of modern motor vehicles, desert explorers should still have some basic tools and repair skills. At the top of the list are tire tools. Make certain your jack, tire irons, and everything you need for changing a flat tire are in good shape. You should also have a tire pump, either electric or manual, which can save the day if you have a slow leak. A can or two of emergency tire inflator/sealant can also be useful.

Carry a small tool kit with several sizes of screwdrivers, pliers, a set of open end wrenches, and a couple of adjustable wrenches. Extra motor oil is a good idea. If your engine's fan belts and radiator hoses are field replaceable, you might consider carrying spares. Jumper cables are always a good idea. Make certain you have spare fuses of the type and sizes used by your vehicle.

Always have a fire extinguisher on board, because a vehicle fire in a remote area could not only deprive you of your transport but all your water, food, and shelter at the same time.

A small but sturdy shovel is essential for digging out a stuck vehicle. You should also carry a tow chain or heavy-duty tow rope. Consider also a set of sand mats, which are heavy pieces of old carpet used to gain traction in sandy areas. Jack platforms, 12-inch squares of heavy plywood used under jacks in sandy areas, are also useful. For trucks and SUVs, a high lift jack is much better than the stock jack.

Water and Food

Since you have a vehicle to carry the load, there's no excuse for not carrying plenty of water. Consider that you'll need water not only for drinking but also for washing cookware and for refilling your radiator if the engine overheats. Again, I recommend dividing your water among a number of smaller containers, rather than relying on one or two large containers.

Food isn't as important as water, but even on day excursions you should have something along. On multiday desert trips, pack food for a couple of extra days in case of delay or breakdown.

Vehicle First-Aid Kit

It's a good idea to take a first-aid course occasionally to stay up to date. You'll also want to have a good first-aid kit in your vehicle, tailored to your specific needs. The following list should be considered a minimum:

- ❑ tweezers
- ❑ needles and thread
- ❑ safety pins
- ❑ magnifying glass
- ❑ single-edge razor blades
- ❑ scissors
- ❑ bandages
- ❑ medical tape
- ❑ roll of gauze

- ❑ gauze pads
- ❑ cotton-tipped swabs
- ❑ moleskin
- ❑ Ace bandage
- ❑ water purifying tablets
- ❑ antiseptic
- ❑ aspirin or equivalent
- ❑ first-aid booklet

Safety in Numbers

Traveling in groups of two or more is safest for several reasons. There's more labor available if your vehicle becomes stuck. In case of breakdown, a couple of people could go for help while the rest stay with the vehicle. There are also more people to look for water and set up camp.

I break my own rules and travel alone, sometimes to pretty remote areas. But I make all the preparations noted earlier, and a few more. I make certain a reliable person knows my plans, knows exactly when I'm due to return, and when and whom to call to initiate a search. In addition, since I'm an experienced desert backpacker, I always make sure that I'm prepared and equipped to walk out. Normally, it's best to remain with your vehicle unless you know that a search won't be mounted, but I feel much better on solo trips knowing that I can walk out if necessary. Naturally, I would not walk out in extreme heat.

Travel in Convoy

When planning a trip to the remotest desert areas, strongly consider traveling in a convoy of two or more vehicles. You not only have a spare vehicle in case of a breakdown but you also have more carrying capacity for water and other supplies.

Hazards of the Road Less Traveled

In addition to flooding (see Chapter 4), you also have to be concerned about several other road hazards. Deep sand can stop even a 4WD vehicle, and quicksand is especially troublesome. Quicksand forms when water from a spring or other

A friend and I were out exploring in his 4WD truck late one summer in the Sonoran Desert when we nearly got trapped by quicksand. We had already been forced to give up on one road that had been completely wiped out by a flash flood at a normally dry crossing, leaving us facing an impossible 10-foot bank where the road had been. Now in the dark, we were trying to cross a broad wash on a maintained, graded dirt road. The wash was running from thunderstorms upstream in the mountains earlier in the day, but the flood had passed and we could see the graded berm along the edge of the submerged roadway just showing in places. Since the water wasn't swift and probably not too deep, I scouted ahead on foot. Sure enough, the water was only a few inches deep and my friend followed behind me without any trouble. On the far bank, I jumped in, and we drove around a gravelly curve and headed across a patch of apparently dry sand that would lead back onto the undamaged, graded road. We both felt the front wheels begin to sink at the same time. Luckily, my friend reacted quickly. He stopped and backed clear while his rear wheels were still on firm gravel. On foot, we saw that our tracks were rapidly filling in. We could walk across the quicksand if we didn't stop, but if I stood in one place the sand around my feet liquefied and I started to sink.

source percolates upward through a bed of sand, partially suspending the grains so they won't support any weight. Quicksand is usually found in small, shallow patches, and it's a minor nuisance to a hiker. But it can thoroughly trap a heavy vehicle.

Dry sand can be coarse and firm, in which case 4WD vehicles will have no trouble with it, and 2WD vehicles can cross short patches, such as washes, without problems as long as you maintain speed. Soft, fine, loose sand can be trouble. Scout ahead on foot to determine how extensive the soft section is. Unless you have another vehicle in your group and a winch or tow chain, be very conservative about making an attempt to cross. If you do get stuck, don't attempt to power your way out; you'll just dig yourself in deeper. You may be able to get moving by rocking the vehicle, that is, shifting from forward to reverse and back again, and gently moving back and forth. If that fails, determine which way and how far to go to get to firm ground, and break out the jack and shovel, as well as sand mats if you have them. Set the parking brake and block the opposite wheel so the vehicle won't roll, and jack up the stuck wheel as far as you can. Fill in the hole with rocks or gravel if available, or sand if not, and then lay out your sand mats under the tire in the direction you need to go. Let the vehicle down, and then gently apply power. Once you get off the sand mats, keep going at the same speed until you reach firm ground. In really soft sand, you may have to unload the vehicle.

You may find mud at creek and river

crossings, on roads during the winter rainy season, or after snowmelt in the higher desert areas. Some forms of mud can stop even a 4WD vehicle, and in all cases, mud makes an incredible mess to clean off back home. Also, driving on muddy roads does a great deal of damage to the roadway. It's a good idea to find an alternate route or go somewhere else rather than trying to power your way through deep mud.

River and creek crossings should be approached with caution. Just a foot of swift water can pile up against a vehicle and sweep it away. Check the depth and firmness of the crossing on foot. If the water is too muddy, deep, or swift to wade, then it is not safe to cross by vehicle. Consider also that water more than axle deep greatly shortens the life of wheel bearings and may splash onto your ignition, stalling your engine in midstream.

Unmaintained roads develop deep ruts and high centers; the ridge between the two main ruts can get so high that the undercarriage of the vehicle scrapes or hangs up, which can do a lot of damage and get you severely stuck. Drive low-clearance vehicles to one side or the other to keep the tires out of the ruts and avoid the high center.

Rocks in the road can do serious damage to tires and underbody parts in short order. Avoid sharp rocks, and make sure you'll clear before driving over a rock. In some cases, it's worthwhile to move rocks by hand, especially to get past a bad spot. Know where your vehicle has its highest clearance. It's generally not in the center but rather on each side of center.

Before driving down a hill, make sure your vehicle can get back up if need be. Even if you plan to exit by a different route, there may be a worse spot ahead that forces you to turn back.

Avoid traveling cross-country except in an emergency. Even the tracks of a single vehicle last for decades in the desert, and where one vehicle goes many more are sure to follow. There are far more hazards off road, including sharp-tipped agaves that can puncture radiator hoses, brush that clogs radiators, hidden ravines and gullies, and sharp rocks.

The Need for Less Speed

Keep your speed down. High speed is for racetracks. At low speed you can creep over and around obstacles instead of banging into them, and those you do hit will do much less damage. You'll also do less damage to the roadway and the desert. Even if you can only drive at walking speed, you're still carrying far more equipment, supplies, and water than you could on foot or bike.

Fat Tires in the Desert

Mountain bikes are a superb way to explore desert back roads and trails. Although bicycles aren't allowed on national park or wilderness trails and shouldn't be ridden

cross-country in the desert, there are plenty of desert roads and trails that are open (called *double-track* and *single-track* in mountain-biker jargon). Modern bikes have excellent tires, gearing, and suspension, and in the hands of a fit and experienced rider they can handle rocky desert double-track with aplomb. Those riders who live in desert cities or towns can often get to great rides right out their door, and those who don't can use their motor vehicle to reach the start of a great single-track or area to explore.

Desert Bike Riding

Mountain biking on all but the most level and smooth roads is strenuous, and it really helps to be fit. Luckily the best way to stay fit is to ride, but any physical activity such as hiking, climbing, or skiing helps keep you fit for cycling.

You can save a lot of energy by learning good mountain-biking technique. The best way to learn is to ride with more experienced riders. Bike shops in desert cities and towns can hook you up with experienced riders and clubs in the area.

Bikes

Avoid the cheap bikes. The last thing you need is for the frame or another vital component to break miles from civilization. Because desert trails tend to be rocky and sandy, you want good tires designed for soft surfaces, and a bike with at least a front suspension to cushion the rocks. A full-suspension bike is really the way to go. Bikes are evolving rapidly; I suggest that you buy and equip your bike at a cycle shop run by experienced desert riders. Most desert cities have at least one such shop.

A mountain bike used for riding in the land of many spines must have thorn-resistant tires and tubes. A liquid sealant in the tubes saves a lot of grief. I once got seven punctures in the same tube in a matter of minutes. Luckily I had a spare tube, but after that I never rode in the desert without sealant in the tires.

Clothing

Avoid cotton clothing. Cotton soaks up your sweat nicely, but then stays wet. If the weather turns cool and windy, cotton makes you a hypothermia victim just waiting to happen. Rescue teams in the Pacific Northwest put it bluntly, "Cotton kills." A wide variety of synthetic cycling clothing that wicks moisture away from your body and dries quickly is readily available in stores specializing in outdoor sports. The same layering system that works well for hiking and mountaineering works well for desert mountain-biking as well. (See Chapter 6 for more information.)

Opposite: The desert has special challenges for mountain bikers, such as boulders and cactus spines just looking for a tire to trash.

Repair

Carry at least one spare tube, preferably two, as well as a patch kit and tire tools. You'll also need a tire pump. Bring a tool kit with tools appropriate to your bike. For extended rides that last several days or more, you'll want a more extensive repair kit, with parts like spare spokes, extra tubes and tires, and brake pads. Usually a sag wagon (support vehicle) is used to carry tools and parts for extended rides, as well as water, food, and camping gear. It's also possible to equip your bike with racks and panniers and travel independently.

Water and Food

What, water again? Yep. And I'm going to give you the same advice. Carry and drink plenty, even in cool weather. Remember, desert air is dry and your skin loses more moisture than you think. Hydration systems are popular because you can drink without stopping. You can also add a hydration reservoir to an ordinary pack. Just make certain you get a system with a big reservoir, holding at least 2 liters. Many hydration systems are designed for short rides in humid country and are just too small for desert use. Of course, you can always supplement your hydration system with water bottles.

Traditional cycling bottles attach to the frame at various points. Oversize bottles are available, and depending on your frame, you may be able to carry 2 or 3 liters or more on the bike. The main advantages of traditional bottles are that your water supply is divided into multiple containers, and the low mounting keeps your center of gravity low.

On one extended desert ride, I was faced with the need to carry water for an overnight dry camp. Since I needed about 8 liters, I attached a rack and panniers to the front wheel and loaded each pannier with a water reservoir filled as full as would fit in the pannier bag. The low center of gravity really helped on the rutted, rocky roads during the first part of the ride.

Another option for multiday rides, at least on double-track, is to cache water ahead by vehicle. But if you're going to do that, you might be better off with a sag wagon.

You'll burn lots of energy riding in the desert, so you'll want high-energy food. You can bring traditional trail munchies or any of many brands of energy bars. Just make sure you avoid ones that melt, except possibly in winter.

Chapter 8

Hiking and Camping in the Desert

I have been a hiker ever since I can remember, and walking is still my favorite way to explore the desert. After the long-approach drive or ride, it's always wonderful to strike out on my own two feet. Walking, whether on a day hike or a 10-day trek, offers the most freedom and puts me in the closest touch with the desert.

Fit and Ready

As with any other physical activity, being physically fit adds greatly to your safety and enjoyment while hiking. I'm not much for gym workouts or running, so I try to do as much hiking and mountain biking as possible in between longer trips. When a long trip is looming, I try to do harder day hikes with bigger loads. Occasionally I succeed. (Auxiliary gear, like photographic equipment or rock-climbing gear, is an effective way to bulk up your pack.) All forms of exercise are helpful in preparing you to carry a heavy load, but the most effective way to prepare to carry heavy loads is to carry heavy loads, which is difficult to do on a day hike. So most of us start a long trek somewhat out of shape for the task. That's why it's important to start easy on the first few days of a long hike. If the approach drive is long, you could camp at the trailhead, if possible. Another tactic is to plan to arrive at the

Backpacking on the Tonto Plateau, Grand Canyon, Great Basin Desert

trailhead during the early afternoon and walk just a few hours before camping. It's awfully tempting to rush the first few days of an exciting trip that you've been anticipating for weeks or months. Even experienced desert hikers fall into that trap. You'll find the remainder of the trip to be far more enjoyable, though, if you take it easy at first. By the third day, you'll find that muscles and mind are adjusting to their new task, and you can cover more ground. This leads directly into planning your trek.

Planning

Foot journeys require more planning than any other mode of desert travel, simply because you're dependent on the supplies and equipment you can carry on your back and, critically, on far-flung desert water sources. Water sources control desert backpacking. Ideally, you want to plan your hike to pass by at least one spring, tank, or other desert water source per day. This doesn't mean you have to camp at water sources, as long as you are practiced at dry camping and have sufficient water-carrying capacity. Ideally, I like to pass by a water source late in the after-noon, so I can tank up on water for a later camp without having to carry it too far. That way I get all the benefits of a dry camp without having a huge load. Of course, the desert doesn't always cooperate with my desires.

Look carefully at your proposed route, using maps, guidebooks, and the ad-vice of friends or rangers who've been there before. Most desert wilderness has few trails, and those that do exist may be poorly maintained and faint. Traveling such trails is always slower than walking a well-manicured trail. Carrying a pack loaded for overnight or longer on a good trail, I plan for a rate of 2 miles per hour, then I add 30 minutes for each 1,000 feet of climbing. That's admittedly conservative, and I almost always do better. Rough, steep trails will slow you down, and if you have to spend time finding the trail you'll make even less progress. Cross-country hiking can slow you to a rate of 0.5 mile per hour or less. Another factor often overlooked is that a group must travel at the speed of its slowest member. Trying to force someone to go faster than their natural pace inevitably results in unhappy people and is also a frequent cause of injury. Remember, you're out in the desert

Madera Creek, a rare permanent stream in the Sonoran Desert

wilderness to enjoy the place, not rush through it to prove how fast you can hike. If you want to hike fast, make sure you go with other like-minded hikers and not with people who may have more contemplative goals on a hike.

Along that line of thought, make sure you allow time for side hikes, photography, wildlife viewing, rock hounding, botanizing, birding, and other such things that you or members of your party may be interested in. And allow some extra time in case adverse weather slows you down.

Water

As you probably realize by now, locating water sources is one of the desert's biggest challenges. With general trip planning, look at maps and guidebooks and talk to experienced hikers and rangers in advance of your trip. Even with the best written or verbal advice, never depend on a single source of water. Always have a backup plan in case a spring, tank, or creek is dry. I once had to turn back from a planned week-long trip in a desert mountain range when an intermittent stream turned out to be dry. The stream was an integral part of my plan to do a long loop hike. When I found out it was dry—unusual for that time of year—I returned to my last good water source, a spring. Since there was no way to complete the loop, I shortened the trip and saved the long loop for another time.

Always keep desert water sources clean and take only the water that you need and will use. This is especially important with rain pockets and rock tanks. In the desert, wildlife absolutely depends on such water sources for survival, and the next hiker will also need them. Never, ever wash up or bathe in a spring or tank. If you're camped near water (remember that state law in Arizona and other states prohibits camping near springs), clean yourself and cookware and answer the call of nature 200 feet away from the water.

Lightness and Being Safe

All things being equal, the lighter your pack, the more enjoyable the walk. Most backpackers carry too much stuff—there's the old joke about the hiker with 500 pounds of ultralight backpacking gear. At the other extreme, some hikers travel far too light in a single-minded quest for the lightest possible load. You have to carry enough shelter and clothing to handle known extremes of weather in the area you'll be trekking through. Likewise, you have to carry enough food and water to maintain energy and hydration while performing strenuous exercise. And finally, you need a first-aid and repair kit to deal with such injuries, illness, and gear breakdowns that are reasonably possible on your trip. The basic rule of gear planning for backpacking is to take everything that you need but look very hard at things you want, and then relentlessly look for ways to lower the weight of every single item.

Opposite: La Ventana Arch, Cebolla Wilderness, New Mexico

Have a Backup Plan

Always have a backup plan in case you encounter a dry water source, an injury, or bad weather. If you've planned your trip too tightly, anything that slows you down can turn the trip into a desperate race to reach the trailhead before a search is started. Look at alternate routes, a shorter loop perhaps, or a place where you can exit the wilderness early, in case you are not making the rate of progress you planned.

Situational Awareness

Pilots use a term called *situational awareness* to describe the technique of staying aware of the big picture. Hikers should use situational awareness too, because it increases both your safety and your enjoyment. Instead of plodding along the trail head down, glance around occasionally. You may pick up the first towering cumulus clouds that presage a violent thunderstorm later in the day. Or you may spot a perfect cactus flower on the shady side of a rock. And you'll certainly be more aware of animal and bird activity, as well as being more likely to spot a coiled rattlesnake or the fresh track of a mountain lion.

Keep aware of your progress toward your next goal, whether it's the next spring or the destination of a day hike. Sometimes it helps to note your progress on the map, which allows you to make a visual estimate of your progress. For example, if you've been hiking for 5 hours, the sun sets in 6 hours, and you haven't reached your day-hike goal, you should turn back within the next half hour in order to reach the trailhead by sunset—assuming you can hike back just as fast as you hiked in. Or say that on a multiday trip you've planned to reach a final spring an hour before sunset, so that you can pick up water for a dry camp. If by lunchtime you aren't halfway to that spring, start making alternate plans. You may want to pick up water sooner, if possible, or camp short of your original goal.

Keep aware of clouds, wind, and other weather signs, such as temperature. They give you valuable clues to approaching weather changes. For example, in the North American Desert high cirrus clouds overrunning the sky during the winter may mean that a rain storm is coming. The early morning appearance of turreted altocumulus castellatus clouds during the summer is often the first warning of thunderstorms later in the day. A southwest wind shifting to the south and strengthening during the winter and spring is often the first sign of an approaching cold front, which not only brings cooler temperatures but may also bring rain or snow. There are many excellent books on weather, and reading through a few will help you understand and use weather signs. See the Recommended Reading list for some examples.

Desert trails are commonly marked with small rock piles called cairns. When the trail is faint, cairns may be your only guide to staying on route. Always make certain you have the next cairn in sight before losing sight of the last.

Travel Techniques

Hiking is not just putting one foot in front of the other. There are definite techniques that can be learned with practice. Just watch a nonhiker on a typical rocky desert trail. He stumbles into rocks, steps on them, and generally makes awkward progress. The experienced hiker, in contrast, seems to always place her feet on the smoothest spots, while effortlessly avoiding ankle-twisting loose rocks and slippery ground, all the while thinking about something else entirely. What's happening here is that the experienced hiker has gained muscle memory and has memorized the pattern of desert trail obstacles so that she hikes along without having to think about her footing. Of course, the rougher the ground, the more conscious effort is needed to traverse it.

Your goal should be to put out a constant amount of effort as the grade and difficulty change. Your overall effort should be sustainable for many hours, or at least the length of your day hike. This means slowing down for hills and rougher sections and speeding up for smooth or level sections of trail.

Daydreaming is an important skill, especially when crossing the inevitable sections that aren't that interesting as well as for long uphill pulls. Once you have some experience, your subconscious scans ahead for hazards such as cactus burrs or rattlesnakes, while your conscious mind is free to think about that delicious camp meal you have planned for the end of the day.

Siesta

If the days are trending toward the hot side, plan to hike early in the morning and late in the evening, and spend the hottest part of the day in the shade. You'll use a lot less water while being able to enjoy the desert when the light is at its best and the air is relatively cool. Using this technique, I often start hiking as much as 45 minutes before sunrise, when there is just enough light to see. I stop by late morning and lounge around in the shade, eating a very leisurely lunch and doing a bit of reading, catching up on notes, and often, taking a South American-style siesta. I may wait until as late as 5:00 P.M. before setting off again. Longer summer days make it possible to put in a full day's hiking even with such a long break.

Gray fox, Arizona-Sonora Desert Museum

Night Hiking

Under the right conditions, night hiking can by very enjoyable, as well as safe. With a bright moon and a smooth trail, you can often move along as quickly as you can during the day. Sometimes you can even hike cross-country, such as across a salt flat or through an area of sand dunes. Even if you only have starlight, there's often enough light to see. Of course, you can use a headlamp to follow a trail at night, but if you have to use artificial light, you're cutting yourself off completely from the beautiful desert night. Instead, use your light sparingly, shielding the beam so as not to destroy your night vision. Once you've adapted to bright light, it takes up to an hour to regain your night vision.

Night hiking is most useful during the fall, when the days are rapidly growing shorter. By hiking for a couple of hours after sunset, you can sometimes reach a desirable campsite or spring that would otherwise be out of reach.

Use extreme caution when hiking on warm nights, because rattlesnakes are likely to be active. Unless the ground is smooth and light-colored, such as salt or sand, it's much safer to hike with a bright headlamp.

Going Your Own Way (Cross-Country)

There are two major differences between following a trail through the desert and hiking cross-country. As you proceed, you must keep track of your location—no more drifting along until you fetch up against a trail sign. And you must grapple with the details of routefinding, which can be easy on an open, sparsely vegetated plain, or it can be close, sweaty work as you make your way through brush or scramble up a broken cliff band.

Keeping Track of Your Position

As you walk, you should keep track of your position by looking at land-marks, such as hills, mountain peaks, rock outcrops, and the like, and then noting your position on the map in relation to those landmarks. For intricate cross-country work, you will probably want to keep the map in an outside pocket so you don't have to remove your pack to check the map. Rest stops are a good time to use the map to note your position, estimate your rate of progress, and check for any obstacles or unusual landmarks coming up. If you have a GPS unit, use it to determine your position and enter any future waypoint you will need. Of course, you can also triangulate your position with map and compass, but you shouldn't need to do this on a routine basis if you keep track of your location as you go.

You should also keep an eye on your back trail by noting, for example, where you crossed a wash or found a break in a short cliff. That way, you can retrace your steps if the way ahead is blocked or just plain unappealing, or if you run out of time or water.

Finding Your Way

Cross-country routefinding becomes easier with experience. General experience always helps, but there's no substitute for knowing the country you're in.

Bahadas

At the foot of many desert mountain ranges, gravel and sand wash down from the steep slopes above and spread out to form a vast, sloping plain that skirts the mountains. Often this bahada extends to the valley floor and meets the bahada from the adjacent range. From a distance, bahadas look like featureless slopes, but up close it's usually a different story. The dry washes that transport all the debris during rare floods usually are incised deep into the bahada surface, sometimes as deep as 100 feet. Though the intervening ridges are usually flat-topped, the washes may make travel on the contour, parallel to the foot of the mountain range, extremely tedious. In contrast, travel directly up or down a ridge is usually easy, often so much easier that it's best to descend one ridge and ascend another rather than try to work your way directly across.

The washes are tempting but usually offer slow going in deep sand and gravel. They often branch in confusing ways, and most of the time you can't see any landmarks. Narrower washes can be choked with brush and boulders.

Slickrock

From a distance, an area of slickrock looks like a daunting navigational challenge. Domes and fins of bare sandstone dot the landscape and appear to be randomly placed. On closer inspection you'll find deep crevices, canyons, and potholes that impede progress, especially in a straight line. The key to understanding slickrock is that it's all drained. Rain and snowmelt inevitably run down the bare rock surfaces and gather in small drainages. These drainages coalesce into larger and larger drainages, which in turn feed into washes and canyons. In the most famous slickrock region, the Canyonlands country in the far eastern Great Basin Desert of southeast Utah, nearly all of the drainage from the slickrock eventually ends up in the Colorado or Green River.

Because slickrock topography is created and defined by drainage, it also has a corresponding series of intervening ridges. Small ridges lead uphill to larger ridges, and these in turn lead to summits and plateaus. It's true that on a local scale the ridges may be interrupted by impassable domes and cliffs, but the general scheme holds true.

You can use this knowledge to find your way through slickrock country. In a torturous landscape such as The Maze in Canyonlands National Park, the canyon bottoms are the best travel routes. Although there are hundreds of tributary canyons, they eventually join into larger canyons and then drain into the Green River, creating order from apparent chaos.

On the east side of Canyonlands National Park, the Needles District is a land of towering fins and graben valleys. Joint cracks, sometimes dozens to hundreds of feet high and just a few feet wide, split the sandstone walls. But again, drainage and canyons connect the entire landscape together. Once you begin to see that pattern on the ground, then the slickrock landscape starts to make sense.

Canyons

Canyons split the slopes of the parallel mountain ranges in basin and range country, in portions of the Great Basin, Mojave, and Sonoran Deserts. The high plateaus of the eastern Great Basin Desert are cut by so many canyons that the country is referred to as Canyonlands. Some canyons offer easy walking, while others are narrow and blocked by dry (or sometimes wet) waterfalls and plunge pools. The skills needed to traverse the most difficult canyons draw heavily on rock climbing and mountaineering techniques, and the term *canyoneering* is often used to describe this activity. Canyoneering is best learned from someone experienced, and technical canyoneering is beyond the scope of this book.

There are many easier canyons that require nothing more than wading and maybe floating your pack on an air mattress across occasional deep pools. When the weather is warm, wet canyons are delightful places to hike.

Canyons are created by floods, and the danger of flooding is something to be considered before entering a canyon. Find out from guidebooks, maps, rangers, or people who've hiked the canyon whether or not there are places where you can escape a flood. Check the weather forecast, and never enter a narrow canyon if there's any chance of flooding. Your first such mistake is likely to be your last.

Always camp above the flood line, even if it means moving on through the canyon in a single day. Even wide canyons flood, and often the last high-water mark is littered with driftwood and other debris.

Ridge Running

Ridges usually offer easier going than the neighboring washes or canyons. You can see where you're going more easily, especially going uphill. Even if a cliff blocks the ridge, you can usually find a way around without too much difficulty. Some desert ridges are so rocky or serrated that travel is slow and tedious, and it's better to follow the drainages.

Desert Summits

Most desert summits can be reached by walking and scrambling, and many peaks offer outstanding views of 100 miles or more in the clear, dry air. It's no wonder that desert peak-bagging is popular.

Take a good look at the peak with binoculars before you start the ascent. Look for cliff bands that may be troublesome. Often there are rock slides that provide a way through. To determine the height of a distant cliff, look for familiar plants such as agave or juniper. Also look into the ravines. Some are straightforward, others are choked with brush and fallen boulders. Check these features against your map and make notes to help you remember which way to go. Once you start up the steep slopes, your view is foreshortened and features may look different or be completely hidden.

Brush
High desert ranges may have dense brush, especially on north slopes. It's usually easier to travel across south- or west-facing slopes, but sometimes you have to make your way through the brush. Some brush is truly impassable, but usually there are openings that aren't apparent from a distance. The trick is to link these openings with a minimum of brush crashing. It's worth taking detours to stay in the openings. Of course, you'll want to wear a long-sleeved shirt and pants, and you may want a pair of leather work gloves.

Pinyon-Juniper Woodland
Found at higher elevations in the North American deserts, pinyon-juniper woodland is a mixture of small juniper trees and pinyon pines, which grow in open stands. PJ, as it's often called, is easy to walk through because the trees usually have plenty of space around them. The main difficulty is navigation. PJ stands are just high enough, usually about 10 to 20 feet, to obscure your distant view. Usually, you can use the sun to stay on course despite the constant small detours. Often there's a slope, which you can use to determine the correct direction by referring to your map. If the ground is flat and the sun hidden by clouds, you may have to walk a compass or GPS course to your destination.

Sand—Quick and Otherwise
Quicksand is found where water seeps into sand from below, buoying up the grains. As you approach, quicksand often appears to be an ordinary patch of damp sand, but as you walk across it, your weight causes it to liquefy, and you start to sink—especially if you stop. Fairly common along canyon bottoms where there is an intermittent flow of water, quicksand is usually shallow, and you can easily walk across. In the few cases where the quicksand is deeper, you can find yourself sinking with each step, until your efforts to extract one foot just cause the other foot to sink deeper. The solution is simple. Get rid of your pack, and then topple over on your face to distribute your weight evenly and "swim" out. You won't sink because quicksand is actually quite dense. You get stuck standing upright because all your weight is concentrated on your feet and exerts more pressure than the quicksand can support.

Ordinary sand is more of a problem because its looseness can make for slow going. Walk as flat-footed as possible and avoid digging your toes or heels in. Slow down and maintain a steady pace. If you're following a canyon bottom, look for damp or crusty sand, which is usually firm and can give you a break from the slog.

Lava and Cinders

Lava flows and volcanic fields are found throughout the North American deserts. You should avoid crossing a lava flow if at all possible, because the surface is usually broken and unstable, and the lava rock is sharp and very hard on footwear. If you do have to walk on lava, watch very carefully for crevices and unstable blocks of rock. Some lava flows are associated with cinder fields, and there may be patches of cinders that make for easier going.

Cinders are usually firm and easy to walk on when you're on the flats, but cinder cones and slopes can be loose. Take advantage of any brush or vegetation that may be growing on the slopes, because the roots anchor the cinders and the ground is usually stable on the uphill side.

Camping

Desert camping is a joy because the weather is usually stable and the views are often spectacular. You won't often be camped near a lake or a gurgling stream, but the desert makes up for the lack of water in other ways. In this section, I'll discuss lightweight camping—the style you have to use when backpacking and that's often desirable when vehicle camping because of its simplicity. Most of these techniques are aimed at "wild camping," where you are free to pick your own site, but many of them are useful in places where you are required, or might prefer, to use a developed campground.

Dry Camping

Desert camps are usually dry camps. Even if there is a spring nearby, state law usually prohibits camping close to a spring, tank, or other isolated water source so that desert wildlife won't be scared off from getting a vital drink. If the law is silent on the subject, you should still avoid camping close to such isolated water sources to avoid the possibility of contamination. Dry camping has several advantages. By not being tied to a water source, you're free to camp nearly anywhere. You can camp in little-used spots and avoid the camp-robber animals that are so annoying in popular campsites. You can camp on ridges, mesas, and mountain tops and enjoy hundred-mile views and awesome sunsets.

Dry camping does take some getting used to because you don't have an infinite supply of water for washing up dishes and yourself. With a little practice, though, you'll be surprised how little water you need for washing. To wash a pot, first scrape it as clean as possible with your spoon. Then use a tiny amount of water and just a drop or two of biodegradable soap. Use a mesh-type pot scrubber, instead of a dishcloth or sponge. The mesh absorbs very little water and dries quickly. For years I used a piece of mosquito netting, but it was olive drab, an effective camouflage color, and I kept losing it or having it blow away in the wind. Now I use a coarser mesh scrubber from the supermarket. It cleans better than the netting, and the 0.25-inch holes let me hang it on a bush to dry, where it seems to stay

Even in the mountains, the technique of dry camping is worth learning, because you can camp in uncrowded, undisturbed spots. (Gila Wilderness, New Mexico)

put even in a strong wind. Clean any spoons and other utensils at the same time.

After the pot is clean, pour out the mildly soapy water and rinse with just a tablespoon or two of water. Rinse your utensils at the same time. Repeat a couple more times. Repeated rinses with a small amount of water are actually more effective than a single rinse with more water. If you've used margarine or the pot is otherwise greasy, heat the wash water on your stove. I usually use the water left over from making after-dinner hot drinks.

This same procedure can be used on cups, bowls, and plates, if any. Make sure you dispose of the dirty water well away from your campsite. You don't want to tempt the innocent local wildlife into becoming camp pests.

I used to hike in barbaric mode and rarely wash up. Of course, the reek in my sleeping bag was pretty overpowering after a few days. Nowadays I find it very refreshing to clean up once a day, if water and time permit. I usually carry out this ritual in the evening unless the weather is cool, in which case lunch is a better time. I bring along a 4-inch square cut from a larger camp towel. These camp towels are made from a spun polyester/nylon blend or rayon viscose, and the material is light and dries quickly.

You can easily brush your teeth using only a couple of tablespoons of water. The trick is to use a very tiny amount of toothpaste.

Even if you are vehicle camping and can carry plenty of water, dry camping techniques will stretch your supply so that you don't have to replenish your supply as often, in many cases saving a long trip to the nearest town.

Minimum-Impact Camping

There are just too many of us enjoying the desert backcountry to indulge in old-style heavy-impact camping. Plan to leave your campsite as you would like to find it, with as little trace of your presence as possible. With modern equipment—

nearly bombproof tents, warm sleeping bags, and comfy sleeping pads—you can camp in comfort and safety without having to modify your site. Durable surfaces such as slickrock, rock slabs, gravel, and sand are all practical campsites that show few impacts from use. Self-inflating foam pads let you camp on coarse gravel or bare rock in comfort, so there's no need to scrape a sleeping surface smooth. Instead, just pick out loose pebbles and sharp objects.

Avoid grass and vegetation as much as you can. All plant life has to struggle to survive in the desert, and although that green, soft carpet of late winter grass looks tempting, it will probably not recover from being crushed under your groundsheet or your boots. Don't remove plants or dig drainage ditches to "improve" your site. Instead, pick a campsite that is naturally drained, as explained in the next section.

Carry out all of your trash. If you carried it in, whether by vehicle, bike, or backpack, you can carry it out empty. When you leave camp, look the ground over carefully for tiny bits of litter—twist ties, bits of foil from food packages, and the like. Over time, these little pieces add up and help give a campsite that hammered look.

Campfires should not be built in the desert. Fires are responsible for more slob campsites than any other bad practice. With good equipment, you can easily stay warm without a fire—and have the added benefits of being able to enjoy the desert night and avoid burning holes in your gear. If you have to build a fire because of an emergency or other good reason, see the "Leave No Trace" section for pointers on minimizing the damage.

Typical dry wash in the Sonoran Desert

Choosing Your Site

Whether you plan to spend just one night in a backpacking camp or establish a vehicle base camp for several days, put some effort into choosing your site. It can make all the difference to your comfort and your mood.

Microclimates are variations in the weather over distances of a few feet or tens of feet. Understanding how this works can make or break your choice of a campsite. The most important microclimate effect is the nighttime temperature inversion, which occurs on clear, calm nights. As the sun sets, the land starts to cool by radiating its stored-up heat to the night sky in the form of infrared waves. The air then cools in contact with the ground. Because cool air is heavier than warm air, it starts to move downhill. As it collects in valleys and drainages, the layer of cool air gradually grows deeper. The air on nearby slopes and ridges stays warmer. The temperature difference can be 20 degrees F or more. Many times I've walked up out of a shallow drainage and noticed a sudden temperature rise just 10 or 20 feet above the bottom. You can take advantage of this effect by camping on ridges or small mesas when you expect the night to be cold.

Wind breaks up the inversion and results in nighttime temperatures that grow colder with increasing elevation. If the air is dry, as it usually is in the desert, the temperature drops by about 5 degrees F for every 1,000 feet of elevation gain. In chilly, windy weather, you should hike high and camp low for the warmest camping. You'll also want shelter from the wind, behind the lee side of cliffs or boulders. Even the sturdiest of tents are more pleasant to sleep in when they aren't snapping in the wind.

Inversions don't form on cloudy nights, because the ground doesn't radiate to the relatively warm clouds.

Your tent, or your sleeping bag if camping under the stars, also cools off by radiating infrared heat to the clear night sky. If you're expecting a clear cold night, look for an overhanging rock or a tree to camp under. Even the sparse branches of a paloverde tree help block the cooling radiation, and denser trees such as juniper and pinyon pine do an even better job.

Pay close attention to your campsite's natural drainage if rain is threatening. Even the best tent floors are going to let water in if you camp in a pond! Choose an absorbent, slightly tilted surface such as sand or gravel or, in the high desert, pine or juniper needles. The slight tilt causes surface water to run off instead of collecting under your tent. If you're expecting a deluge, try to find ground that is slightly dome-shaped so that water runs away from your tent in all directions. Failing that, a slight ridge works well. Of course, the surface must still be level enough for sleeping.

Although gravel or rock slabs are good campsites if you have a comfortable self-inflating sleeping pad, they present challenges when it comes time to anchor a tent or tarp. Soft sand is also a problem. If the ground is too hard for your tent

Once I was on a 5-day hike in the Sonoran Desert during a very wet winter. Storm after rain storm passed through the Southwest, with a couple of sunny days in between. On this occasion I'd been hiking in the rain most of the day, but the sun came out briefly in the afternoon. The trip was a delight—all the normally dry washes were running deep and clear, just like mountain creeks, and there was green grass everywhere, and even a few flowers. You have to be a desert rat to truly understand just how glorious that was.

As the sun sank in the west and I started looking for campsites, it became clear that it was going to rain hard and long. I found a site on a slightly sloping ridge that was protected between some bushes and boulders, and I set up my tarp and groundsheet. I sloped the foot end of the tarp low to the ground and faced the open head end away from the wind and pitched it close to the bushes for additional protection. Sure enough, the rain came pouring down well before dark and continued for hours. I, however, was completely snug, dry, and warm under the tarp. Water poured off the edges and ran down the sloping ground away from my groundsheet on both sides. In the morning, I found that the ground was flooded in low-lying spots. It had rained at least an inch, possibly more.

stakes, anchor guy lines to rock outcrops, bushes, or trees if available. To anchor the corner of a tent floor, or a guy line where there's nothing to attach to, lay the stake flat on the ground, at right angles to the direction of pull, and stack one or more large rocks on top. In soft sand, push the stake in vertically, then place a large rock on top of the stake, or on the guy line just in front of the stake.

After all my dry-camping talk, water is nice if you have it. A campsite with a nearby spring or creek is always a special treat in the desert. Just remember to camp at least 0.25 mile from any isolated spring, out of consideration for wildlife. And never do dishes or wash up in a spring or creek or within 200 feet of open water.

Consider where the sun will rise when you locate your campsite. In cold weather, it's very pleasant to have the sun strike your tent or sleeping bag just when you have to face getting dressed. In warm weather, you'll want to be in the morning shade as long as possible—especially with a tent, which can become an oven in direct sun. You can measure the bearing of sunrise with a compass on the first morning of your trip, or just use the general knowledge that the sun rises directly east on the spring and fall equinoxes (March 21 and September 21), and in the North American deserts, it rises about 30 degrees farther south in midwinter (December 21) and about 30 degrees north in midsummer (June 21).

If you're camping under trees, watch out for widow makers. These are large branches that can come crashing down and write a very unhappy ending to your expedition. Cottonwood trees that are found along desert washes and streams are weak and commonly lose huge branches in windstorms.

Of course, once you've satisfied all the requirements above, it's still not a perfect campsite unless it has a sweeping view of the distant mountains or at least a spectacular, jagged skyline.

Cactus and Self-Inflating Pads

If you use an air mattress or self-inflating pad, look over the ground very carefully before laying out your tent or groundsheet. Dead spines and burrs blend into the desert ground. In twilight, shine your flashlight horizontally across the ground, which helps spines stand out. Never put a self-inflating pad directly on the ground—tent floors and ground sheets offer at least some protection. If I'm really worried about cactus spines I haven't found, I spread out a fleece jacket or other article of spare clothing under the sleeping pad for extra protection. If you're car camping, you can carry a closed-cell foam pad to put under your self-inflating pad for added protection and comfort.

Just at sunset, a friend and I walked into a well-used but still very pretty Sonoran Desert campsite in a canyon bottom with clear pools of water and the echoing sound of croaking frogs and canyon wrens. It had been a long day and we were looking forward to dinner and a fine night under the stars, but even before we had our ground sheets laid out a striped skunk ambled out of the bushes and nonchalantly checked us out—no fear! Knowing our peaceful night was a goner, we stuffed our groundsheets back in our packs, broke out our headlamps, and started hiking. An hour later we were on a beautiful, rocky ridge with a fine view of the mountains and level spaces just big enough for our sleeping bags. We got our peaceful night—a gentle breeze, no bugs, and no skunks.

Camp Robbers

When a campsite has been used by large numbers of people, it often develops a large animal camp following as well. These squirrels, skunks, mice, ringtail cats, and birds get used to the easy pickings and can become very annoying. The best defense is to avoid heavily used campsites, especially slob campsites with fire rings full of half-burned trash and litter lying around. Failing that, there are some defensive measures you can take.

If you're vehicle camping, store your food in your vehicle in coolers and boxes. Backpacking camps are more of a challenge. Keep your food in stuff sacks and hang them up when not cooking or eating. A tree branch is ideal but, failing that, you can run a nylon cord between two boulders and hang your food sacks from that. You can hang your food from the overhanging side of a boulder or small cliff, or make a tripod from walking sticks or agave staves or the like. Try to hang your food at least

> *Food left out even for a moment can be fair game. A couple of friends and I were camped near the Colorado River in Grand Canyon on a 12-day hike. Sleeping sites were tough to come by and we were spaced about 50 feet from each other. In the morning, with my pack partially packed and some daytime munchies sitting on the top, I walked away to get some water from the nearby side canyon. A shout caused me to turn as a raven swooped smoothly down on my pack, plucked a bag of homemade beef jerky from my snack bag, and flapped away. A few minutes later, as we resumed our hike, we passed the raven and a buddy perched on a huge boulder finishing the last of my delicious jerky. At least the thief shared with a friend!*

10 feet off the ground, because of skunks and ringtail cats. Mice especially are very clever at breaking down your defenses. They can climb down stuff-sack cords and gnaw through the toughest nylon, given time. Luckily, it usually takes mice a couple of nights to figure out your methods, so campers who camp in lightly used sites and move each day present a more difficult, moving target.

Empty your pack of all food, snacks, and trash, and leave the pockets open. That way mice and ringtails can check things out without having to chew their way in. Cook and wash up away from your tent and sleeping site, if possible, and never leave food in your tent.

Another approach to the pest problem is to stop and have dinner well before reaching your campsite. That way, you're separating your cook and sleep areas by a large distance.

Note that I'm not talking here about the ultimate camp robbers—bears. Grizzly bears are extinct in the North American deserts, and black bears are only found in the forested mountains above or adjacent to the deserts. You may encounter black bears in such areas, but usually they are very shy of humans.

Never, ever feed wildlife! You are not doing animals and birds a favor by feeding them. Human food is not good for them and you are creating camp pests dependent on human handouts or leavings.

Spring Wildflower Hikes

Bull Pasture, Organ Pipe Cactus National Monument
Hugh Norris Trail, Saguaro National Park
Willow Spring Trail, Mazatzal Mountains
Peralta Trail, Superstition Mountains
Picacho Peak, Picacho Peak State Park
49 Palms Oasis, Joshua Tree National Park
Barnhardt–Rock Creek Loop, Mazatzal Mountains

Chapter 9

Surviving the Worst

When things go wrong, it's nice to have a few options. As a pilot, I always make sure I have a "back door"—a way out in case of bad weather, and a landing strip in mind in case of mechanical problems or an ill passenger. It should be the same with your desert treks. Don't use all your water in base camp before driving out for more. Don't rely on a single spring when backpacking—always have a plan to backtrack or go to an alternate source if there's no water. Pace your group at the speed of the slowest member. Decide in advance how you will get help if someone gets hurt on a long, remote hike. In general, if you use common sense you can avoid or minimize most desert problems.

When emergencies do arise, they are usually a matter of surviving the next few hours or at most several days. Long-term survival, where you have to live off the land, is a thing of the past in the North American deserts, where you are never more than 2 days' walk from a road or a town. (In some other desert regions of the world, long-term survival is still a possibility, though greatly diminished by modern tools, such as satellite navigation and communication.)

In this section, I'll discuss from a common-sense point of view what to do in a desert survival situation, using the equipment and skill you already have or will develop from desert camping, hiking, and biking experience. I'll leave living off roots and rattlesnakes to the survivalists, who are the only ones who practice such skills enough to have them at hand when needed.

Leave Plans with a Reliable Person

The importance of this rule struck me when I was on a solo hike in some very rough terrain. I realized that if I got hurt and couldn't hike out, no one would know where I was, at all. I'd driven a couple of hundred miles from my summer job on a U.S. Forest Service fire lookout, then traveled 30 or 40 miles of back road. My vehicle would eventually be found, but that would still leave hundreds of square miles of desert to search. By not leaving word of my plans I was being selfish and needlessly thoughtless of my family, friends, and the rescue team.

You can leave word with a family member, a friend, or a ranger, but the chosen person must be reliable and must thoroughly understand what he or she is supposed to do, and when. I give my backup person a written itinerary, or preferably a map with my route and possible alternate routes clearly marked. Whichever method I use, the date and time that I plan to be out is always clearly specified. My instructions always say that I will be in contact by that time, and if not, that the backup person should wait a specified time, usually 24 hours, before contacting rescue authorities. I also give the phone number of that rescue authority, which is generally the county sheriff in the American desert areas, except for the national parks, where the rescue authority is the National Park Service. Once you set that deadline for yourself, make absolutely certain that you meet it.

I'm writing from a solo perspective, because many of my desert trips are solo, out of necessity. However, it's just as important for groups to leave word of their plans as well. Doing so will save a lot of anxiety if someone gets hurt on the trip or can't keep up. That way, the group leader will know that help will come at a certain time, which is comforting knowledge even if the group has the resources to deal with the problem.

Lost

Being a "mite confused" about your location is scary, especially the first time it happens to you. (It will happen—trust me!) All of a sudden the trail is gone, or an expected landmark doesn't appear when it should. Often the first impulse is to Do Something! But the best reaction is no reaction. Sit down, have a drink of water and some munchies, and think about the situation. After all, even if you're lost now, you weren't just a short time ago. Go over your recent route in your mind and see if you can mentally retrace your steps to a known point. Ninety-nine percent of the time you can figure out where you went wrong, and simply retrace your steps to find the trail or a familiar point.

In the rare event that doesn't work, carefully note your stopping point, then search carefully out and back from it, looking for a trace of the trail, rock cairns, tree blazes, or other trail markers. Look at the map and decide where the trail would have likely gone. If you don't find the trail in a reasonable distance, come directly back to your original stopping point and then search out in a new direction.

If there's still no trace of the trail, but you can find a landmark on the map near the trail or route, and also confidently identify that landmark in the landscape, you can head for the landmark in hopes of finding the trail there. In this case, though, you had better be prepared to proceed along your planned route cross-country because the trail may have faded out for good. A common situation is where a trail follows a broad wash by staying up on the alluvial banks most of the time, crossing the wash at bends. It's easy to lose the trail at the crossings, and you may choose to stay in the wash and pick up the trail where it crosses later on. Of course, you should be ready to turn back if the wash becomes too rough and the trail never reappears.

Many desert trails are marked with rock cairns, and sometimes little-used trails are so faint that the cairns are the only thing keeping you on track. If you lose the cairns, too, walk back to the last cairn and search out from it, looking for additional cairns. Keep in mind that the trail may have taken an unexpected sharp turn. This technique also works with trails marked with tree blazes or plastic stakes.

As a last resort, you can always walk out to your baseline, as described in Chapter 5.

Injury

A disabling injury on a wilderness trek strands at least some of the party while the remainder goes for help. Never leave the victim alone, unless there are just two of you and there's no other choice. Signaling for help is very much preferable to leaving a victim alone. Ideally someone can stay with the victim and two can go for help, but in groups of three the person sent out will be hiking solo. Make certain both groups' intentions are clear, preferably written down, before they separate.

The person or group staying with the injured person should set up as comfortable a camp as possible, keeping in mind potential changes in the weather, and be alert for approaching rescuers, and prepared to signal if necessary.

Stranded

If your vehicle breaks down or becomes hopelessly stuck on a remote back road, your best choice is nearly always to stay with the vehicle, which is much more visible to searchers than are people on their own. Only consider hiking out if you know that no one will come looking for you, and you have the water, food, equipment, and experience to undertake the walk. Most inexperienced people vastly underestimate the difficulty of walking out. All it takes is one serious blister to bring you to a halt, now miles from both your vehicle and help.

If your vehicle has been in an accident, fire, or is otherwise damaged, first secure your supplies of water, food, and equipment. Then have some members of the party set up camp while others go about signaling for help.

Signaling Techniques

If you have a cellular phone, by all means give it a try. Don't be too surprised, though, if it doesn't work. The cellular phone companies provide coverage to cities and major highways where there is a large market. Especially if you are in a valley or canyon, you are likely to have no signal. On the other hand, if you're on a ridge or can easily get to one, you may be in range of even a distant cellular system, especially if you can see a major highway or city. Be prepared to tell the 911 dispatcher your exact location, nature of the problem, and assistance required.

Another high-tech signaling method that works nearly anywhere is the personal Emergency Position Indicator Radio Beacon (EPIRP). These use the same search-and-rescue (SAR) satellite systems as the ELTs carried in aircraft, and the satellite operation center can quickly determine your location after you activate the EPIRP. Some EPIRPs have built-in GPS and transmit your exact position, saving even more time. You might want to consider carrying one in really remote deserts, especially outside North America. If you plan to be in very remote territory, renting a satellite phone would make sense. These work anywhere you have a clear view of the sky.

Don't overlook lower tech but proven signaling methods. Internationally, SOS, whether sent by Morse code (...- - -...), spoken on a radio, or marked in huge letters on the ground, is the universal distress signal. In North America three of anything is the distress signal. That includes three smoke columns, three fires, three gunshots, three flashes from a flashlight or headlights, or three blasts on a whistle. Such signaling is especially useful when you've spotted searchers, but they have yet to spot you. Since it's difficult to sustain a signal fire in most deserts, if you are able to find enough wood and green vegetation to build three smoky fires, keep them unlit until searchers are near.

Signal mirrors are very effective in sunny weather. Mirror flashes can often be seen over 100 miles in the clear desert air. Glass signal mirrors with a targeting grid are best, but any mirror will do in a pinch. With a signal mirror, all you do is sight through the hole and put the lighted spot on the target. With a vehicle side mirror or other plain mirror, hold your thumb at arm's length, place the tip on your target, then sight over the edge of the mirror and bring the flash down to the tip of your thumb. With either kind of mirror, tap it with a finger to set up a flashing and twinkling that will draw the target's attention. If the sun is low behind you, have someone stand in front of you with a second mirror and reflect the sun to the signal mirror. Most American desert areas are regularly crossed by both airliners and lower-flying small aircraft, so in good weather it shouldn't take too long to get someone's attention.

Once a pilot has clearly spotted you, you need some way to communicate your problem. Ground-to-air signals were developed for just this purpose. Lay the symbols out with any contrasting material—pieces cut from plastic ground sheet, or even toilet paper weighted with stones, and make them at least 10 feet wide. As a

Ground to Air Signals

LL	All well	**☐**	Require map and compass
N	No	**F**	Require food and water
Y	Yes	**X**	Unable to proceed
⌐L	Not understood	**I I**	Require medical supplies
→	Am proceeding in this direction	**I**	Require doctor
K	Indicate direction to proceed	**SOS**	International distress symbol

last resort, scrape aside the surface soil to make them, which will create at least some contrast.

Pilots who are not specifically trained in search and rescue may not recognize all of the ground-to-air signals, but all will understand SOS. Since the next response to your distress signals is likely to be made by trained searchers in fixed-wing aircraft, you should lay out the appropriate ground-to-air signals in advance of their arrival.

A rescue aircraft can answer by rocking its wings to indicate signal received and understood, or by making a right 360-degree turn to indicate signal received but not understood.

In remote areas, the actual rescue may be carried out by helicopter, especially if there are injuries. You can greatly assist the pilot by setting up a wind indicator, such as plastic or cloth strips tied to the top of an agave stave or other mast. Failing that, you can give the pilot a good indication of the wind by throwing a double handful of loose dirt into the air when the helicopter is on final approach. Also note any hazards, such as powerlines or other hard-to-see wires. Stay well clear of the nearly invisible main and tail rotors, and approach the helicopter only when signaled to do so by a crew member.

Finding Water

To stay alive, you need water, shelter, and food—and water is by far the most important in the desert. You can stay alive for weeks without food, but in hot weather without water, your survival time is measured in hours. Shelter from the sun is also far more important than food.

If you need water in an emergency, consider first the cost in sweat and energy of searching for water, especially in the heat of the day, against staying put and resting in the shade. It's not only cooler and the light less glaring in morning or evening light, but animals and birds move to water at that time and may help you find it.

There are three main sources of water in an emergency: groundwater, such as

springs, creeks, and intermittent creeks; trapped runoff, such as water pockets, rock tanks, and plunge pools; and man-made sources, such as wells, guzzlers, stock tanks, and watering troughs.

In the desert, groundwater tends to come to the surface where there are topographic or geologic breaks, such as at the foot of mountain ranges or at outcrops of hard, impermeable rock layers. Unusually green vegetation often accompanies a spring, and washes where groundwater is close to the surface are often lined with water-loving trees, such as cottonwoods, willows, ashes, and sycamores. Even though there may be no surface water during midday, often some appears by early morning each day, especially in bends and low spots in the bed. This occurs because streamside vegetation uses less water at night.

Water pockets form on large, level expanses of sandstone, where standing rainwater dissolves the calcite cementing the sand grains together, deepening the pockets—sometimes to amazing depths that hold water for months after a storm. Look for water pockets on top of large boulders as well.

Rock tanks and plunge pools form in normally dry washes where bedrock has been exposed and then eroded by swirling floodwaters to form a deep basin in the rock. Tanks, or *tinajas* as they are also called, can hold anywhere from a few cups to many thousands of gallons. In some desert regions they are the only reliable water source. Look upstream from the mouths of desert canyons, especially steeper canyons. Wildlife activity is often a strong clue. Rock tanks often form in a series along a favorable stretch of canyon, so don't give up if the first one you encounter is dry.

Artificial water sources are built by ranchers and wildlife managers in many desert areas. Drilled wells in remote desert regions usually have a windmill, storage tank, and water trough. If the trough is dry, check the steel tank for water by feeling for coolness at the water level and below. You may find a valve, or possibly can lower a pot on a cord through an opening in the top. If all else fails, you may be able to start the windmill, if the wind is blowing, by releasing the control handle wired to the tail fin. It's usually found about head height on the tower.

Guzzlers collect rainwater, usually for wildlife, and have a collection area of plastic or concrete that feeds into a storage tank and a trough. The collection area can be seen from above at a fair distance, so if you are on a ridge or can get to one, scan the bahada or valley below you.

Stock tanks are built by ranchers to provide water for livestock, by bulldozing a small earthen dam across a wash. Sometimes dikes or channels are built to funnel more runoff into the reservoir. Like guzzlers, stock tanks are generally built on gently sloping terrain, so if you can get to a high point, scan the slopes below.

Opposite: Cottonwood—the tree of life in the desert. This riparian tree provides welcome shade and only grows where groundwater is near the surface. Surface water is often found nearby along the drainage.

Rock tanks along a wash, seen from above. Look carefully or you may miss this important water source. One pool is below the boulder at the upper left and another is beyond the small saguaro at the lower right.

A couple of friends and I had planned a week-long hike through some slickrock country where the only water sources would be water pockets and rock tanks in the drainages, aside from one spring near the start. It had been several weeks since the last wet weather, so we weren't sure what we would find. Other trips through similar terrain had always revealed more water than expected, so we started off optimistic.

After filling our bottles at the spring, we reached the first of the slickrock terraces where we might find water pockets about midmorning. The other two set off on a side hike to climb a butte, while I searched for water along the sandstone ledges, terraces, and canyons. After hours of searching, I'd found nothing. Every single water pocket was dry. When my friends returned, they reported the same result on their route. Reluctantly, we gave up the trip and retraced our steps to the spring. If we had continued our original hike, we might have found water, but we might not—and then we would have been in real trouble.

Looking toward the sun early or late in the day can help, because the small ponds reflect the water. Close up, the muddy, trampled, defecated-in water may not be appealing, but your water purification system will make it safe. If you don't have any purification system but have a water emergency, you'll have to risk getting sick—which is better than the alternative.

Ranchers also place watering troughs at strategic locations and fill them by water truck, especially in times of drought. Never use water from these troughs except in an emergency.

Shelter

If the weather is hot, you need shelter from the sun. By staying in the shade and resting through the heat of the day, your body consumes far less water and energy than it does if you're in the sun and active. Carry out physical activity during the cool of morning and evening, or at night.

The best shade is that of a dense tree, such as a cottonwood, or an overhanging rock ledge. Of course, in a desert survival situation you're not likely to have either. A tarp, pitched well above the ground for air circulation, works well provided the material isn't too thin. Ultralight nylon tarps can be doubled to better block the sun. A space blanket, which is highly reflective, also makes a good sun shade. A tent, even one with a fly, pitched on the ground is an oven in hot sun. Instead, pitch the floor just as if it were a tarp, with the loose canopy on top.

If you're stranded in a vehicle without camping gear, stay in the shade of the vehicle, crawling underneath if necessary. You may have to dig a depression under low-clearance vehicles to do this. Of course, make sure the parking brake is set, and chock the wheels with rocks.

In cold or stormy weather, you need protection from wet and wind. If you have camping or backpacking gear, see the "Camping" section in Chapter 8 for tips on setting up a secure camp in a storm. If you have no gear, one option is to stay in your vehicle and run the engine for warmth. Always leave a window slightly open to guard against carbon monoxide poisoning from the exhaust. Without an operable vehicle or if you've lost your camping gear, find the most sheltered location you can. The lee sides of small cliffs, alluvial wash banks, boulders, and overhanging ledges work well. If firewood is available, build a fire that will reflect its heat off the rock behind you. Huddle together for warmth. Space blankets are very effective for their weight because they protect you from wind and rain while reflecting your body heat back.

Food

In a hot-weather survival situation, eat sparingly unless you have plenty of water. Metabolizing food uses water, and you can survive for weeks without food. The opposite applies in cold weather, where you need food to maintain your body's ability to produce heat. You need to drink and eat to avoid hypothermia.

Desert Peaks

Wheeler Peak, Great Basin National Park
Spirit Peak, Newberry Mountains
Picacho Peak, Picacho Peak State Park
Matterhorn Peak, Jarbidge Mountains
Superstition Peak, Superstition Mountains
Quartz Peak, Sierra Estrella
Mount Ellen, Henry Mountains
Mount Tukuhniqivatz, La Sal Mountains
Mount Ajo, Organ Pipe Cactus National Park
Mount Wrightson, Santa Rita Mountains
Telescope Peak, Death Valley

Resources

Land Management Agencies

National Park Service
Pacific West Region
Regional Director
One Jackson Center
1111 Jackson Street, Suite 700
Oakland, CA 94607
(510) 817-1300
www.nps.gov

U.S. Bureau of Land Management (BLM)
Arizona State Office
222 North Central Avenue
Phoenix, AZ 85004
(602) 417-9200
www.az.blm.gov

California State Office (BLM)
2800 Cottage Way, Suite W-1834
Sacramento, CA 95825-1886
(916) 978-4400
(916) 978-4416
TDD: (916) 978-4419
www.ca.blm.gov

Nevada State Office (BLM)
1340 Financial Boulevard
Reno, NV 89502
(P.O. Box 12000, Reno, NV 89520)
(775) 861-6400
Fax: (775) 861-6606
www.nv.blm.gov

New Mexico State Office (BLM)
1474 Rodeo Road
Santa Fe, NM 87505
(505) 438-7400
Fax: (505) 438-7435
www.nm.blm.gov

Oregon State Office (BLM)
333 SW 1st Avenue
Portland, OR 97204
(P.O. Box 2965, Portland, OR 97208)
(505) 808-6002
Fax: (505) 808-6308
TDD: (505) 808-6372
www.or.blm.gov

Utah State Office (BLM)
P.O. Box 45155
Salt Lake City, UT 84145-0155
(801) 539-4001
Fax: (801) 539-4013
www.ut.blm.gov

U.S. Forest Service (USFS)
Intermountain Region
324 25th Street
Ogden, UT 84401
(801) 625-5306
www.fs.fed.us/r4

Southwestern Region (USFS)
333 Broadway SE
Albuquerque, NM 87102
(505) 842-3192
www.fs.fed.us/r3

U.S. Fish and Wildlife Service
Southwest Regional Office
500 Gold Avenue SW
Albuquerque, NM 87102
(505) 248-6911
http://southwest.fws.gov/

State Parks
Arizona State Parks
1300 West Washington
Phoenix, AZ 85007
(602) 542-4174
www.pr.state.az.us

**California Department of Parks and
   Recreation**
1416 9th Street
Sacramento, CA 95814
(P.O. Box 942896, Sacramento, CA
   94296)
(800) 777-0369
(916) 653-6995
Fax: (916) 654-6374
info@parks.ca.gov
www.parks.ca.gov

Nevada Division of State Parks
1300 South Curry Street
Carson City, NV 89703-5202
(775) 687- 4384
Fax: (775) 687- 4117
http://parks.nv.gov

New Mexico State Parks
P.O. Box 1147
Santa Fe, NM 87504
1-888-NMPARKS
www.emnrd.state.nm.us/nmparks

Oregon Parks and Recreation
   Department
725 Summer Street NE, Suite C
Salem, OR 97301
(503) 986-0707
www.prd.state.or.us

Utah State Parks
1594 West North Temple
Salt Lake City, UT 84114
(P.O. Box 146001, Salt Lake City, UT
   84114)
(801) 538-7220
parkcomment@utah.gov
www.stateparks.utah.gov

Weather and Climate
National Climatic Data Center
http://lwf.ncdc.noaa.gov/oa/ncdc.html

National Weather Service
www.nws.noaa.gov

Unisys Weather
http://weather.unisys.com/index.html

Weather Underground
www.wunderground.com

Maps

DeLorme
www.delorme.com

Maptech
www.maptech.com/

National Geographic Topo! Maps
http://maps.nationalgeographic.com/topo/

TerraServer
http://terraserver.microsoft.com/

Topozone
www.topozone.com

U.S. Geological Survey Topographic Maps
http://store.usgs.gov/

Recommended Reading

Campbell, Charles. *Backpacker's Photography Handbook*. New York: Amphoto, 1994.

Fleming, June. *Staying Found: The Complete Map and Compass Handbook*. Seattle: The Mountaineers Books, 2001.

Fletcher, Colin, and Chip Rawlins. *Complete Walker IV*. New York: Knopf, 2002.

Gardener, Mark. *Photography Outdoors: A Field Guide for Travel and Adventure Photographers*. Seattle: The Mountaineers Books, 1995.

Grubbs, Bruce. *Desert Hiking Tips: Expert Advice on Desert Hiking and Driving*. Guilford, CT: Globe Pequot/Falcon, 1999.

_____. *Using GPS: GPS Simplified for Outdoor Adventurers*. Guilford, CT: Globe Pequot/Falcon, 1999.

Letham, Lawrence. *GPS Made Easy: Using Global Positioning Systems in the Outdoors*. Seattle: The Mountaineers Books, 2003.

McGivney, Annette. *Leave No Trace: A Guide to the New Wilderness Etiquette*. Seattle: The Mountaineers Books, 2003.

Meyer, Kathleen. *How to Shit in the Woods: An Environmentally Sound Approach to a Lost Art*. Berkeley: Ten Speed Press, 1994.

Miller, Dorcas S. *Backcountry Cooking: From Pack to Plate in 10 Minutes*. Seattle: The Mountaineers Books, 1998.

_____. *More Backcountry Cooking: Moveable Feasts by the Experts*. Seattle: The Mountaineers Books, 2003.

Van Tilburg, Christopher. *Canyoneering*. Seattle: The Mountaineers Books, 2000.

Weiss, Eric. *Wilderness 911: A Step-by-Step Guide for Medical Emergencies and Improvised Care in the Backcountry*. Seattle: The Mountaineers Books, 1998.

Wilkerson, James A. *Medicine for Mountaineering & Other Wilderness Activities*. Seattle: The Mountaineers Books, 2001.

Woodmencey, Jim. *Reading Weather: Where Will You Be When the Storm Hits?* Guilford, CT: Globe Pequot/Falcon, 1998.

Glossary

alluvium—Erosional debris such as silt, sand, gravel, and rocks transported by occasional floods and otherwise dry washes and deposited in desert valleys.

azimuth—A direction expressed in degrees clockwise from north.

backcountry—As used in this book, an area accessible only by dirt roads. See *wilderness*.

bahada—A sloping plain extending from the foot of desert mountain ranges to the level desert floor. The bahada is created by outwash debris (see *alluvium*) from numerous washes that fan out from the mouths of mountain canyons. Sometimes the lower edges of bahadas from parallel ranges meet so that the resulting desert valley has a broad V shape.

bearing—The direction, in degrees clockwise from north, from your location to a distant landmark or destination.

cairn—A small pile of rocks used to mark a trail.

campground—As used in this book, an official, developed campsite. In some desert backcountry areas, such as most national parks, camping is allowed only in campgrounds. Campgrounds vary widely in the type of facilities provided. Some just have designated sites, fireplaces, and picnic tables, while others have showers, RV hookups, restrooms, a store, and some added attraction, such as a man-made lake.

course—The line you intend to travel to reach your destination.

declination—The difference, in degrees, between true north and magnetic north at a given location.

double-track—Mountain biker's term for an unmaintained road. Cars and trucks create two parallel ruts, and the rut you're not riding in at the moment is always the smoother of the two. Double-track ranges from easy, nearly level riding on a firm, packed surface to deep, loose sand to steep, rocky, eroded jeep trails.

fault—A fracture in the bedrock caused by movement of the rock layers. Erosion of the shattered rock creates breaks in otherwise impassible cliffs. Desert routes often take advantage of faults.

flash flood—A sudden rise in water level in a stream, or the sudden arrival of water in a normally dry wash, usually caused by a thunderstorm or other sudden, heavy rain. Flash floods are usually thought of as a wall of water, but usually the flood contains such large amounts of silt, sand, and even boulders that its consistency can be more like a debris flow.

GPS—The Global Positioning System, also known as Navstar. GPS is a system of 21 operational satellites in 12,000-mile orbits, plus orbiting spares and ground control stations. The system is operated by the U.S. Department of Defense and is freely available to all users internationally. A small, lightweight receiver picks up the signals from four or more satellites and calculates your exact position.

graben—A valley created by sinking of the valley floor between adjacent mountains or ridges. Death Valley is a famous graben—sinking is the only mechanism that could have lowered it below sea level.

guzzler—A system that collects rain water, stores it in a tank, and keeps an open water trough filled. Normally constructed for wildlife such as bighorn sheep.

inversion—Colder air trapped beneath warmer air, common in desert valleys and canyons on clear, calm nights.

landmark—A physical feature of the landscape, such as a distinctive peak or mesa, used for navigation.

microclimate—Local variations in weather over distances of tens or hundreds of feet.

playa—A large salt flat or dry lake bed that may hold a seasonal lake.

position—Your current location, which can be expressed as coordinates in a GPS receiver or as a mark on a map.

rain pocket—See *water pocket.*

ripstop—A taffeta-like fabric woven with a larger thread at small intervals, in both the warp and weft directions, forming a closely spaced grid. These stronger threads help stop rips from spreading, while keeping the ripstop fabric lightweight.

rock tank—A natural water catchment basin in bedrock, usually carved out at the base of dry waterfalls by floods. Rock tanks may hold just a few gallons of water or many thousands of gallons. See *tinaja* and *water pocket.*

single-track—Mountain biker's term for a trail created by bicycle, foot, or pack animal. There's only one tread. Switchbacks, loose sand and gravel, and rocks and boulders create some of the most technical and difficult riding.

slickrock—No one is exactly certain how this term got started, but it's now used to describe bare sandstone desert terrain, which is common in southeastern Utah and other sandstone desert areas. In the desert, under the combined action of water and wind, sandstone often erodes into rounded shapes. From a distance, these domes and other soft-looking terrain features merge smoothly together. Close up, the sandstone surface is rough and complex, creating demanding terrain with a high-friction surface much enjoyed by mountain bikers.

spring—A place where underground water reaches the surface. Some springs are seasonal and only flow during a wet season, and others are permanent, normally flowing year-round.

stock tank—A small reservoir created behind an earthen dam. Ranchers build stock tanks for their domestic stock, especially cattle.

sun protection factor (SPF)—A rating for sun-protective clothing and sunscreen. Sunscreen rated at SPF 15 is approximately 15 times more protective than bare skin.

taffeta—A smooth fabric woven from identical yarns in both directions.

tinaja—A rock tank that holds seasonal or permanent water. See *rock tank* and *water pocket*.

wash—A desert watercourse that is dry except during floods. Such floods can be caused by a storm too distant to see and may occur with little warning.

water pocket—A natural water catchment that holds rain or melted snow after a storm. Water pockets are found in large areas of bare rock, especially on sandstone. They are usually smaller than rock tanks, ranging in volume from a few cupfuls to hundreds of gallons of water. Large water pockets may last for months after a storm, but small ones can dry up in hours or days. See *tinaja* and *rock tank*.

water saver—Same as a *guzzler*.

waypoint—A position or location, expressed in coordinates and stored in a GPS receiver or marked on a map. A waypoint can, but doesn't have to, correspond to a landmark.

wild camping—Camping at large, in undeveloped sites. Wild camping is permitted in many desert backcountry areas, such as those administered by the Bureau of Land Management, but prohibited in others, such as some national parks.

wilderness—A roadless area. The Wilderness Act of 1964, under which the National Wilderness Preservation System is governed, defines wilderness as a contiguous roadless area in which the effects of humans are essentially unnoticeable. Motorized recreationists often use *wilderness* and *backcountry* interchangeably, but I will use wilderness to refer to roadless areas only. See *backcountry*.

windmill— A well pumped by wind power, usually installed by ranchers for domestic stock.

Index

4WD vehicles 50, 125
A Africanized bees 79
agave 41, 71
aircraft 157
air mattresses 113, 151
alpine packs 108
amusements 119
anchoring a tent 150
animals 72
ankle support 102
artificial water sources 159
autumn 65
winter 65
avoiding cactus 71
B backup plan 140
bahadas 32, 143
baseline 90
bears 152
bees 79
bike repair 133
bikes for the desert 133
binoculars 99
bivy sacks 114
black widow spider 77
boiling water to purify 62
breathable fabrics 105
brown recluse spider 77
brush 145
C caching water 58
cactus 69
campfires 19, 116
camping 18, 146
camp robbers 151–52
campsite drainage 150
camp stoves 116
candelilla 39
canyons 144
car keys 118
carrying water in your vehicle 57
carrying water on foot or bicycle 57
cellular phones 156
centipedes 78

chemical water purification
Chihuahuan Desert 22, 39
chlorine dioxide tablets 62
cholla cactus 69
choosing your campsite 149–51
climate and elevation 64
clinometer 88
closed-cll foam pads 111
clothing 104
collapsible water bottles 58
compass work 88
cone-nosed bugs 78
contour lines 86
convoys 129
cook gear 116
coordinate systems 93
copperhead snakes 76
cotton 104
coyotes 30
cross-country hiking 142
cross-country routefinding 143
cryptobiotic crust 18
clothing for cycling 133
cyclometer 96
D datums 93
day packs 108
declination 88
dehydration 81
desert hazards 69
desert pavement 18
desert peaks 162
deserts of the world 21
determining position with GPS 95
differential GPS 93
digital cameras 120
distress signals 156
down 104
driving cross-country 131
driving the back roads 125
driving the desert 49
dry camping 146
dust storms 84

E emergency locator transmitter 156
EPIRP 156
emergency shelter 102
equipment checklist 122–23
external frame packs 109
F feeding wildlife 152
fibers for clothing 104
field guides 49
film cameras 119
find a bearing with GPS 96
finding water 58, 157–59
fire starting 100
first-aid kit 101
fitness 135
flash floods 81
flashlight 100
floods 81, 144
food for survival 161
food storage 152
footwear 102
G gear for the desert 97
Gila monster 76
Global Positioning System 85
Gore-Tex 105
GPS 49, 85
GPS errors 95
GPS for driving 91
GPS receivers 92
GPS when hiking 95–96
Great Basin Desert 24, 34
Great Basin National Park 35
ground-to-air signals 157
groundwater 159
groups 129
guidebooks 49
guzzlers 159
H headlamp 100
heat exhaustion 82
heat hazards 81
helicopters 157
hikes by season 115
hikes for kids 64
hiking and camping 135
how much water 55
human waste 18
hydration 99
hydration packs 108
hydration systems 58
hypothermia 83
I illumination 100
injury 155
inner layer 106
insect repellent 118
insulating layer 106–07
insulation 102
internal frame packs 109

inversions 149
iodine tablets 61
J Joshua tree 31
L land management agencies 163
lava and cinders 146
layering 106
Leave No Trace 16
leave plans with a reliable person 154
LED flashlights 100
light loads 138
loading a pack 107, 110
lost 154
lumbar packs 108
M magnetic north 88
map reading for desert hiking 86
maps 47, 165
map symbols 87
microclimates 149
mines 80
minimum-impact camping 147–48
Mojave Desert 22, 30
Mojave National Preserve 45
Mojave rattlesnake 73
mosquitoes 79
mountain bikes 51, 131
mountain lions 30
moving maps 93
multiday packs 109
N National forests 45
National monuments 44
National parks 44
National preserves 45
National wildlife refuges 46
navigating by the stars 118
navigation 85, 99
navigation for biking 96
net tents 116
night hiking 142
North American deserts 22
North American Monsoon 26
nutrition 101
O ocotillo 30
off-road driving 50
open-cell foam pads 111
orienting a map 86
outer layer 106
outer shell layer 107
P pack construction 109
pack covers 110
pack pockets 110
packs 107–10
pack volume 107
paddling the desert 53
permits and regulations 46
photographic equipment 119–20
photographic techniques 121

pinyon-juniper woodland 145
planimetric maps 86
planning 126, 136
plotting a bearing 89
plunge pools 159
poison ivy 72
pots 117
predators 79
prefiltering water 62
preparation 126
pump microfilters 61
Q quicksand 130, 145
R rattlesnake bites 75
repairing sleeping pads 113
repair kit 101
ridge running 144
ringtail cats 33
river and creek crossings 131
road hazards 129
roadless areas 44
road maps 86
rock tanks 159
rocky roads 131
S safety in numbers 129
saguaro cactus 27
sand 145
sand storms 84
scorpions 77
seasons 64
self-inflating foam pads 113, 151
shelter 113, 161
shin dagger 39
side hikes 138
siesta 141
signaling techniques 156
signal mirrors 156
situational awareness 140
sleeping bags 110–11
sleeping pads 111
slickrock 143
snakes 72
socks 104
solo trips 154
Sonoran coral snakes 76
Sonoran Desert 22, 25
spiders 77
spring 66
spring wildflower hikes 152
State parks 46
stock tanks 159
stranded 155
stuck in sand 130
summer 64
summits 145
sunglasses 100
sunhat 100

sun protection 99–100
sunrise in camp 151
sunscreen 100
sunstroke 82
survival 153
SUV's 49, 125
synthetic fibers 104
T tarantula 77
tarps 114
ten essentials 98
three-season tents 114
tinajas 159
toilet paper 118
topographic map features 87
topographic maps, computer 47
topographic maps 47, 85, 86
tracking your position 142
trail hiking 51
travel techniques for hikers 141
trekking cross-country 51
triangulation 90, 91
true north 88
U unmaintained roads 125
utensils 117
V vehicle first-aid kit 129
vehicle maintenance 128
W walking a compass bearing 89
walking to a baseline 90, 92
wallet 119
waste, disposing of 18
watch 118
water and climate 55
water and food for cycling 134
water for backpacking 138
watering troughs 161
water pockets 159
waterproof/breathable/windproof fabrics 105
waterproof fabrics 105
water purification 61
water sources 58
waypoints 94
weather 66
weather and climate 164
weather forecast 126
weight on your feet 102
wells 159
western diamondback rattlesnake 73
Wheeler Peak 37
widow makers 151
Wilderness Act 43
Wilderness Areas 43
wild horses 39
wind hazards 84
windmills 159
windproof fabrics 105
Y yucca 42

About the Author

Bruce Grubbs is an avid hiker, mountain biker, paddler, and cross-country skier who has been exploring the North American Desert for more than 30 years. He always makes time for several week-long desert treks every year. An active outdoor writer and photographer, he's written 15 outdoor guidebooks, and his photos have been published in *Backpacker* and other magazines. He is also an active charter pilot. He lives in Flagstaff, Arizona. For additional information, check the author's website at www.brucegrubbs.com.

THE MOUNTAINEERS, founded in 1906, is a nonprofit outdoor activity and conservation club with 15,000 members, whose mission is "to explore, study, preserve, and enjoy the natural beauty of the outdoors. . . ." The club sponsors many classes and year-round outdoor activities in the Pacific Northwest, and supports environmental causes through educational activities, sponsoring legislation and presenting educational programs. The Mountaineers Books supports the club's mission by publishing travel and natural history guides, instructional texts, and works on conservation and history.

Send or call for our catalog of more than 500 outdoor titles:

The Mountaineers Books
1001 SW Klickitat Way, Suite 201
Seattle, WA 98134
800-553-4453

mbooks@mountaineersbooks.org
www.mountaineersbooks.org

33 East Minor Street
Emmaus, PA 18098
800-666-3434
www.backpacker.com

The mission of *Backpacker* magazine is to provide accurate, useful, in-depth, and engaging information about wilderness recreation in North America.

MORE TITLES IN THE *BACKPACKER* MAGAZINE
SERIES FROM THE MOUNTAINEERS BOOKS

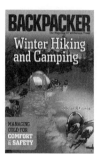

Winter Hiking and Camping:
Managing Cold for Comfort and Safety, *Mike Lanza*
Make the most of your cold-weather experience with the help of a *Backpacker* magazine editor.

Adventure Journal, *Kristin Hostetter*
Be a modern Thoreau! Inspiration and a perfect format for chronicling your outdoor adventure.

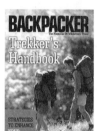

Trekker's Handbook:
Strategies to Enhance Your Journey,
Buck Tilton
Contains pre-trip, during the trip, and post-trip strategies for long-distance hiking.

Hiking Light Handbook:
Carry Less, Enjoy More, *Karen Berger*
Practical, reasonable strategies for everyone who'd like to lighten their load on the trail.

Everyday Wisdom:
1001 Expert Tips for Hikers, *Karen Berger*
Expert tips and tricks for hikers and backpackers selected from one of the most popular Backpacker magazine columns.

More Everyday Wisdom:
Trail-Tested Advice from the Experts,
Karen Berger
More tips for enhancing backcountry trips.

Backcountry Cooking:
From Pack to Plate in 10 Minutes,
Dorcas Miller
Over 144 recipes and how to plan simple meals.